Autobiographical Writing and Performing

AN INTRODUCTORY, CONTEMPORARY GUIDE TO PROCESS AND RESEARCH IN SPEECH PERFORMANCE

Diane E. Howard, Ph.D.
University of Mary Hardin Baylor

The McGraw-Hill Companies, Inc.
Primis Custom Publishing

New York   St. Louis   San Francisco   Auckland   Bogotá
Caracas   Lisbon   London   Madrid   Mexico   Milan   Montreal
New Delhi   Paris   San Juan   Singapore   Sydney   Tokyo   Toronto

McGraw-Hill Higher Education
A Division of The McGraw-Hill Companies

Autobiographical Writing and Performing
An Introductory, Contemporary Guide to Process and Research in Speech Performance

McGraw-Hill's Primis Custom Publishing consists of products that are produced from camera-ready copy. Peer review, class testing, and accuracy are primarily the responsibility of the author(s).

 2 3 4 5 6 7 8 9 0 QSR QSR 9 0

ISBN 0-07-240093-5

Editor: Sharon Noble
Cover Design: John Hancock and Hershall Seals, UMHB Art Professors
Printer/Binder: Quebecor Printing Dubuque, Inc.

To David Richard Howard,

who has supported the author

in every endeavor

for thirty years of marriage

ACKNOWLEDGEMENTS

Pioneer work can be lonely and risky. While initiating new methodologies and applications based on fresh research and experimentation, an innovator appreciates colleagues, friends, and family, who encourage, affirm, and facilitate. Some of the author's supporters have gone out of their way to encourage the research, development, and delivery of the processes and products outlined in this text. Gratitude is above all expressed to Dr. Cecila Erlund of the University of Mary Hardin-Baylor and to Dr. Lucia McKay of the University of Texas at Austin for their guidance, support, and facilitation of the author's original investigations of the significance of role modeling. Gratitude is further expressed to Dr. Lucinda Harman for her statistical evaluation of original and ongoing research. Grateful acknowledgement is extended by the author to administrators and deans at the University of Mary Hardin-Baylor for the following: openness to the development of the methodologies described in this book, travel provisions to national and international performance studies conferences, and summer development leave for continuing research and writing.

Gratitude is conveyed to Dr. Curtis Beaird, Vice President for Academic Affairs at UMHB, for his expressions of interest in and affirmation of the publication of this textbook. Appreciation is expressed to Hershall Seals, chairman of the UMHB Art Department, and to John Hancock, of the UMHB art faculty, for designing the cover of this text. Thanks are conveyed to Kay Daughtery, Anna Loan-Wilsey, and Katrina Bailey for research assistance as UMHB library staff. For editorial support, thanks are given to Amy Bawcom, of the UMHB English faculty.

For facilitation of research at New York University appreciation is extended to Diana Taylor and Joe Simmons, of the Performance Studies Department, and to Pamela Bloom, of the Bobst Library. Gratitude is expressed to Carole Kleinknecht for editorial aid. For facilitation of writing and research in New York City, gratitude to Glen, Carole, and Morgen Kleinknecht is further extended. For providing encouragement and information, thanks is given to performance studies colleagues, especially to Ronald Pelias, Nathan Stucky, Kristin Valentine, Joni Jones, and Lynn Miller. For editorial aid, gratitude is extended to Cynthia Wimmer, Performance Studies International associate.

For research and long-distance programming support, gratitude is conveyed to BellNET (Bell County Network for Educational Technology) staff, researchers, and collaborators. These include Bill Dugas, MaryAnn Smith, and Amanda Prill of Texas Agricultural Experiment Station at Blackland Research Center; Lucinda Harman and Michael Fox of the University of Mary Hardin-Baylor; and Suzzette Chapman, Stan Dyer, Jane Purschbach, and Brad Hinson of Central Texas College. Thanks are conveyed to Marjorie Byers and Sharon Noble, McGraw-Hill editors, for publication facilitation. Gratitude is expressed to Roy Barry and to George Dulaney for legal guidance and representation. For their promotion of this text, gratitude is extended to directors of the Cultural Activities Center of Temple, Texas, especially to David Pennington and Margaret Anne Lara.

For encouragement and affirmation, gratitude is extended to UMHB colleagues, especially to Portia McKown and Nancy Travis. For expressions of interest and encouragement, appreciation is expressed to the author's family, friends, and members of the First Baptist Church of Belton, Texas. Thanks are offered to all, who have prayed for the author.

Special thanks are expressed to UMHB performance studies student and alumni writers/performers, who have participated in and encouraged the development of the techniques outlined in this textbook. For the photograph of Carlotta Russell Maneice as Sojourner Truth, gratitude is extended to AWC Photographs. For support of and participation in the processes described in this text, appreciation is expressed to Matt Howard, broadcast journalist and to Mark Howard, website designer. Thanks are also given to Jon Howard, computer software programmer/designer for marketing consultation. Finally, special gratitude is expressed to David Howard, family therapist, for providing ongoing interest, travel arrangements, and editorial support related to the research, development, and delivery of the processes and products discussed in this guide.

Contents

Part I

Historical Insight

Chapter 1 Effects of Historical, Cultural, and Social Context

Chapter 2 Lessons from the History of Performance

Part II

Choosing and Studying the Character

Chapter 3 Role Modeling

Chapter 4 Researching

Chapter 5 Studying

Part III

Developing the Script

Chapter 6 Writing the Script

Chapter 7 Using Performance Frames

Part IV

Performing the Script

Chapter 8 Performing Subtext through the Body

Chapter 9 Performing the Character's Voice

Part V

Producing the Performance

Chapter 10 Costumes, Props, Set, and Multi-Media Effects

Preface

This text is an introductory guide to researching, writing, and performing autobiography. Broadly approaching the subject, this textbook basically concerns the presentation of oneself or another, from original words of the one presented. These personal communications may have been dictated, transcribed, and/or adapted from interviews or oral histories and/or may have been written by the one depicted, in letters, journals, diaries, or written autobiographies. Writing and performing autobiography, thus defined, would involve one person presenting the personal, verbal or written communication of himself, herself, or of another. Autobiographical forms would include letters, journals, diaries, memoirs, confessions, oral histories, and written autobiographies. Autobiographies, which are historical, spiritual, philosophical, poetical, narrative, descriptive, and/or explanatory in nature, would be included. (Spengeman 1980:xii)

This text provides insight into the unique nature of autobiographical writing and performing. This book does not promote writing and performing *biography*, which emphasizes the recounting of *objective*, external events and experiences of another. Rather, the focus of this text is on writing and performing *subjective* questions, struggles, and representations of self-biography, self-definition, self-representation, self-explanation, self-justification, self-invention, self-illusion, and/or self-disclosure of the writer/performer himself/herself or of the words and life of the individuals being presented. Finally, stories and performances of autobiography are not necessarily linear, chronological, or one-dimensional. They can be presentations of associated montage or diverse collage images about multiple facets of human personality and identity.

Writing and performing autobiography is uniquely beneficial, educational, and therapeutic for both writers and performers and for their audiences. It encourages understanding, compassion, and empathy. Challenging stereotypical images, it discourages hasty judgments, based on simplistic understandings of others. This text presents evidence from the author's research that through its role modeling effect, writing and performing autobiography may influence achievement motivation in audiences. Writing and performing autobiography facilitates valuable insights and skills for writers/performers. It encourages close study of history and aggressive research from first-hand sources. It requires careful study of character, crafted writing skills, careful selection of performance frames, perceptive consideration of non-verbal communication, selective blocking of movement, attentive study of voice, and effective engagement of audiences.

Performances of autobiography over videoconference equipment facilitate open communication in what seems like an atmosphere of anonymity. One-person, autobiographical productions can easily be performed for long-distance audiences. They can also be simply presented to on-site audiences in theatres, museums, schools, churches, and performing arts, cultural, historical, and civic organizations. Performance of autobiography can be pursued as communication art or it may be pursued as an effective, succinct, comprehensive, and contemporary approach to the study of speech performance.

This text has a wide range of uses and applications. Students of speech communication, speech performance, mass communication, performance studies, or theatre can use it as introductory, comprehensive, and contemporary project-based curriculum. It is applicable to studies in related fields, such as history, literature, psychology, sociology, and education. This text provides insight into cultural dynamics, such as that of gender, race, and ethnicity. It is useful in producing solo performances. Finally, this textbook can guide students, researchers, writers, and performers of autobiography.

Part I

Historical Insight

Chapter One

Effects of Historical, Cultural, and Social Context

Introduction

The fields of study of written and performed autobiography are broad. Written and performed autobiographies have emerged in many forms, as there have been limited restraints, models, and rules. In preparing to write/perform such work, it is important for writers/performers to understand how historical, cultural, and social contexts have affected production of such enterprises. Further, writers/performers should seek to understand how gender, race, and performance dynamics have affected this genre. Studying historical autobiographical samples, which have been affected by such factors, can provide important, aesthetic insights for writing and performing contemporary autobiographies.

Effects of the Rise of Individualism

Written autobiographies in Europe emerged at the end of the Middle Ages. As the feudal system disintegrated, so did fixed concepts of individual identity within the social system. Social unrest, mobility, and economic opportunities birthed fresh possibilities for personal identity. Additional developments in science, trade, and travel expanded opportunities for identity and individualism. Individuals found new interest, meaning, and pleasure in everyday living.

The first extant autobiography written in English at the end of the Middle Ages was *The Book of Margery Kempe.* She recorded her personal experiences in the early years of the fifteenth century, leaving a journal of life and travel at that time. She described her pilgrimages to Jerusalem, to Rome, to St. James of Compostella, and to Danzig. She wrote of her spiritual revelations; however, she also honestly wrote of her earthly, human relationships. Her autobiography combined her spiritual chronicle with her factual narrative. Kempe was an anomaly in her time. Sidonie Smith, noted historian of female autobiographies, paraphrased an Emily Dickinson poem, "Margery Kempe tested for her culture the boundaries between madness and divinest sense." (Smith 1978:84) Smith presented some interesting insights about Kempe and her autobiographical work:

> …female religious broke out of the cloister and wandered over the face of Europe. Unattached to male orders, unattached to husbands, these women traversed the public spaces and assumed public voices…But their anomalous and unconventional independence threatened social relations and tested the boundaries of heresy. Margery Kempe, a medieval mystic from a burgher family…left behind a most remarkable story of one such woman's life…Kempe sought to convince her reader and her church that her name belonged in the genealogy of great female saints. She looked back on powerful foremothers for a legitimate and authoritative life script: Maternal narratives thus helped her structure her self-representation… (Smith 1987:60)

Effects of Mirrors and Self-Portraitures

Towards the end of the Middle Ages, new interest in self may have been encouraged by the invention of glass mirrors. This development may have stimulated production of self-portraits, which emerged in the late fifteenth century. As Rembrandt had sought obsessively in more than one hundred portraits of himself for a sense of personal identity, Albrecht Durer, likewise, sought his self-identity in a wide variety of self-portraitures at the end of the fifteenth century. Durer used mirrors to aid his introspection in producing these portraits. Paul Delany, noted historian of autobiographies, observed that

> Durer's self-portraits change radically as he pursues his elusive core of selfhood through various costumes…expressions. The brooding self-portrait at the age of twenty seems to suggest an anxious search for a lost identity. (Delany 1969:13)

In 1559 a *Myrroure for Magistrates* encouraged the idea of recorded personal history as a mirror for readers. In his dedication of the text, William Baldwin wrote

> "here as in a loking glas, you shall see (if any vice be in you) howe the like had bene punished in others heretofore, whereby admonished, I trust it will be good occasion to move you to the soner amendment."
> (Baldwin 1559, in Delany 1969:64)

In 1591, *A Christal Glasse,* the narrative account of the life and death of Katherine Stubbes, was published by Stubbes' husband, as "a mirror of woman-hood [and]…a perfect pattern of true Christianity."(Stubbes 1591) In this text the subject spoke at length in first-person discourse of her personal experience, especially of her imminent death at 20 years old:

> "Christ is to me life, and death is to me advantage: yea the
> day of death is the birth day of everlasting life, and I
> cannot enter into life, but by death, therefore is death the
> door or entrance into everlasting life…This blessed Spirit
> hath knocked at the door of my heart, and my God hath given me
> grace to open the door of my heart, and he dwelleth
> in me plentifully…I thank my God through Jesus Christ, he is
> come… O most holy, blessed and glorious Trinitie, three
> persons and one true and everlasting God, into thy blessed
> hands I commit my soul and body." (Stubbes 1591, in Mascuch
> 1996:57-59)

The reference of a mirror as a metaphor may have originated from the idea of a medieval medical speculum as a reflecting instrument used to assess the internal state of an individual's body. An autobiographical text as a mirror enabled readers to see internal issues in themselves through the subjective experiences of others. Further, recorded personal history was considered valuable for virtuous guidance and instruction. In his 1616 Henry Wright wrote

> "History is auaileable to instruct any private man…how
> to frame his life, and carry himselfe with commendation
> in the eye of the world, when, as in a glasse, he shall
> see how to beautifie & compose it, according to the value
> of other men's virtues." (Wright 1616:71-72,in Delany 1969:65)

Effects of Renaissance Ideals

During the Renaissance, there was new interest in nature and what was natural. Self-representation was more individual, honest, and clarified. The inventions of the telescope and microscope encouraged more attention to details and particulars. The philosophy of Descartes rested on the assumption that pursuit of truth was an individual matter. (Smith 1987:24) Rosseau's philosophy later promoted individual freedom and return to nature. Philosophical autobiography appeared in the eighteenth century. (Spengeman 1980:14) In the nineteenth century, poetic autobiography emerged.

Social mobility and unrest encouraged an interest in recording family histories. There was a regard for classical literature and ancient biographies. Writing was no longer a sole function of clerics. Latin no longer had a monopoly on the recorded word. The vernacular of the day was written. During the sixteenth, seventeenth, and eighteenth centuries in England and in Europe, individuals began to believe that their life stories were worth chronicling. Based on new individual freedom and self-identity, new self-expressions and self-representations emerged. This period of history basically encouraged an autobiographical orientation to life.

Effects of Reformation and Counter-Reformation Ideals

During the sixteenth and seventeenth centuries, a sense of progress and individualism inspired self-representation. A general Christian world-view encouraged the value of every individual. A concept of equality developed from a general belief in equal access to God. The attaining of personal knowledge of God was possible for every Christian. Scrutiny of the inner life encouraged self-examination, self-representation, and personal responsibility. There were opportunities for individual testimonies in Protestant congregations and for personal confessions in Catholic communities.

There was even a place for dramatic preaching and teaching in the published autobiographies of Christian leaders in the seventeenth and eighteenth centuries. Religious autobiographies developed. George Fox, founder of the Quaker Society of Friends, wrote like a prophet. He passionately penned his autobiography in the social context of revolution, civil war, regicide, persecution, and the proliferation of religious sects, which both denounced other groups and pled for toleration for their own. Autobiographies of this period were filled with stories of suffering and imprisonment. (Shea 1968:5)

During the seventeenth century, Christians wrote autobiographies in two dominant forms. One form was more objective and religious in nature; the other was more subjective and spiritual in essence. Religious autobiographies written by Catholics and by Anglicans church leaders typically focused on more objective, external, and historical information. Jesuit priests began to write them early in the seventeenth century. (Catholic laymen usually did not write them.) Anglican Church leaders followed the Jesuits in writing autobiographies. Such works by Anglican prelates were scarce and mild. Like Jesuit autobiographies, they were emotionless, objective, dignified, and reticent. The autobiographies of both groups were *objective* histories of religious events. (Presbyterians and Protestants from other sects wrote more *subjective,* personal, spiritual histories of individuals.)

Jesuits wrote of the *holy war* of the Counter-Reformation, rather than of individual experiences with God's spirit. Forming a spiritual aristocracy, they produced autobiographies, which were sober, emotionless, action narratives of persecutions, narrow escapes, and conversions of souls. Jesuits projected themselves as obedient, discreet, and self-effacing. They wrote autobiographies in Latin at the request of their superiors for the instruction and edification of novices in their order. Jesuit autobiographies included stories intended to inspire bravery, endurance, and cunning in the face of persecution. A Jesuit, Gerard, wrote of interrogation and torture in London at the hands of an anti-Catholic inquisitor:

> "…He spoke from the cesspool of his heart. But his effect on me was the opposite of what he wanted: he raised my hopes…I answered…You can do nothing unless God allows it. He never abandons those who trust in Him…I was hung up again. The pain was intense now, but I felt great consolation of soul…my heart filled with great gladness as I abandoned myself to His will." (Gerard: 1609,in Delany 1969:41-42)

Although Gerard's account revealed his humility, it did not reveal his personal introspection. In his story he projected personal vigor, initiative, and decisiveness that enabled him to endure imprisonment and ultimately to escape. He displayed no fear of martyrdom. In his account he demonstrated extreme devotion to his order, eagerness to convert souls at any cost, and confidence in a heavenly martyr's reward. (Delany 1969: 41-42)

Before 1642 most anti-Anglican religious leaders were Presbyterians. After 1642 many parliamentary supporters split off into other Protestant religious groups. More personal, introspective, spiritual autobiographies were typically written by Presbyterians and by members of other Protestant groups. (Delany 1969:4&55) The practice of daily self-examination often included writing personal experiences in a notebook. This journal was used for spiritual reflection, meditation, prayer, confession, and self-information. Insights worth remembering were recorded. These could reflect the writers' understandings about their spiritual state, worship, prayer, or thoughts for meditation and study. During the English Civil War, Interregnum, and Restoration periods, published spiritual autobiographies were especially important for members of non-sanctioned, religious sects, who were prohibited from congregating. Spiritual autobiographies were motivational, instructional, and edifying to members of non-conformist groups.

By 1650 the voice of real experience was valued for being inspirational. Published autobiographies were popular among English gentry and merchants. Preserving the best instances of personal, spiritual experience was deemed important as testimony or witness. Authenticity was significant as the body of Christian sayings was recorded for the edification of the godly community and for posterity. (Mascuch 1996:63-70) Personal autobiographies by members of persecuted and non-sanctioned groups, which traced the whereabouts and associations of the writers, were written for justification or protection. (Mascuch 1996: 112) Robert Blair, the deposed minister of St. Andrews in England, wrote

> "I think myself obliged to leave some notes concerning the
> chief passages that have occurred to me in my pilgrimage,
> that my wife and children, at least, might have these to
> be a memorial of the way that I kept in the world, and

that they may be the better furnished to answer the calumnies and reproaches that have been, and possibly may be cast upon me." (Blair 1636, in Mascuch 1996:90-91)

The habit of documenting *matters of fact* (apparently a legal phrase related to the recording of actions and movements in order to protect one from false accusation) was expanded to encourage those less vulnerable to attack to keep national records as well as personal ones. John Beadle, an Essex minister, wrote a practical manual for spiritual journals or diaries. Published in 1656, it was entitled *The Journal or Diary of a Thankful Christian.* Beadle urged the recording of public and historical events for national examination, as well as the recording of personal information for self-examination. He wrote that private journals should record national and personal history:

> "Nationall, and more publick…a Stone of witnesse…the Nationall Epidemicall sin of the time…the various and changeable condition of the Times in the Countrey where we live…the severall and most remarkable judgments that God hath in our time inflicted upon notorious offenders, whether persons in high places, or such as moved in lower orb." (Beadle 1656, in Mascuch 1996:113-114)

Effects of Social Position

In the seventeenth century men of rank or social position journalized their secular or professional accomplishments. They recorded, as well, great events, which they had witnessed, or sights they had seen in their extensive travels. Professional soldiers documented battles and sieges. Aristocrats wrote descriptions of court or diplomatic life. (Delany 1969:4) Renaissance autobiographers inherited from antiquity the idea that noble deeds should be recorded and commemorated, even if they were one's own. Military and political memoirs were written for self-vindication, as well as for self-commemoration. They were also designed to stir the reader with the sensuous excitement and action of the writers' colorful and assertive lives. Men of social position often produced autobiographies to impress others of the greatness of their family trees, as well as of their own personal actions, adventures, and accomplishments.

Some men of social rank penned their autobiographies as advice to their descendants. In the seventeenth century Roger North wrote

"...I lay downe for a truth...that the best legacy
parents can leav to their children is good principles
...I shall alledge some few passages of my oune experience..."
(North 1836, in Delany 1969:149)

Aristocratic fathers wrote advice books in first person to their sons to remind the heirs of the family's noble history and civic virtues. These books, which were handed down to succeeding generations, often dealt with concepts of honor, wealth, power, and public service. These texts, which were practical in nature, focused on amassing wealth, on spending, on courtly affairs, and on national and international politics. Such works, with their emphasis on public acts, were published to encourage remembrance and imitation of public service. (Mascuch 1996:93-96)

Some men of social position wrote autobiographies to justify their rise to power and wealth. Some wrote autobiographies to trace their professional careers in scientific fields. Most importantly, recorded personal history of men of social rank and position served to stimulate readers to act heroically to preserve the social and political status quo. (Mascuch 1996:101)

Effects of Print

Prior to the end of the seventeenth century, autobiographies were published primarily in manuscript form. At the turn of the century, autobiographies were available in print. Profound introspection during silent reading was encouraged. Print opened up new and greater personal horizons for individuals. More structure and form appeared in autobiographies. Editing was facilitated. A printed text was considered more organized, substantive, authoritative, and valuable. After the English political and religious upheavals of 1640-1689 and after the Act of Toleration ended persecution, printed autobiographies became more historical in form and content; more personal, specific, and concrete in detail; more chronological in structure; and more narrative in cause and effect order. Most importantly, there was an adherence to plausibility and truth. Proof and verification were important to assure credibility. Title pages used descriptors such as "narrative," "account," "history," instead of "mirror" or "pattern." Preserving truth was of utmost importance. Authentic first-person accounts were considered valuable vehicles of truth. (Mascuch 1996:114-115)

Testimony or profession of faith was important to evangelical Protestants. Therefore, nonconformist, evangelical, religious groups used printed spiritual autobiographies as evangelistic tools. After the 1650s Protestant groups, especially Quakers, recorded personal experience for publication. Quakers established a formal editorial process for autobiographical accounts intended for print. (Mascuch 1996:120-131) They were the most active and prolific of nonconformist religious groups in their use of print to testify, to record, and to teach.

Effects of Gender

Historically, published autobiographies by male authors were more accepted and respected in public discourse. Conversely, published expressions of individual freedom and identity by female authors were not as accepted throughout history. Therefore, the publication of autobiographies was more complex for women than for men. Female autobiographers were more limited and marginalized than were male authors. As females, in general, were pushed to the margins of male-dominated cultures, so were female autobiographies. (Smith 1987:7)

Misch, noted autobiographical historian, made the observation that autobiographers represented the time in which they lived to the degree that they were able to participate in public life:

> Though essentially representations of individual personalities, autobiographies are bound always to be representative of their period, within a range that will vary with the intensity of the author's participation in contemporary life and with the sphere in which they moved. (Misch 1951:12)

Sidonie Smith discussed the problem of female authors as representatives of their time. She stated that the term *representative* was problematic from the perspective of women's experience. She contended that female autobiographers were not characteristic of women of their time. She asserted that a woman's published narrative in 1700's-1900's was not representative:

> Very few women have achieved the status of 'eminent person';… those who have done so have…commonly been labeled 'exceptional' rather than 'representative' women. Perhaps such women and their autobiographies would more accurately be 'unrepresentative'…Or perhaps such life stories, while unrepresentative of women's lives, might be representative of men's lives. (Smith 1987:8)

Women's narratives were outside the boundaries of dominant cultures and outside autobiographical model types, which were primarily male models. The typical scripts of women's lives were determined largely by conventions of patriarchal cultures. Women's struggles for individuality and its expression were impacted by culturally prescribed norms of female identity. Words such as "charming…witty, skillful, polished" were among *appropriate* words used to praise female autobiographies. (Smith 1987:11) Smith argued, however, that such words of praise were narrow, limited, and neither profound nor significant:

> Criteria used to evaluate the success of any…autobiography lie in the relationship of the autobiographer to the arena of public life and discourse. Yet patriarchal notions of woman's …nature and…social role have denied or…proscribed her access to the public space;…male distrust and…repression of female speech have either condemned her to public silence or …contaminated her relationship to the pen as an instrument of power…If she presumes to claim a fully human identity by seeking a place in the public arena…she transgresses

patriarchal definitions of female nature by enacting the scenario of male selfhood...she challenges cultural conceptions of the nature of woman and thereby invites public censure for her efforts. If she bows to...pressure for anonymity, however, she denies her desire for a voice of her own. (Smith 1987:70)

Boys typically identified with males and came to speak with the authority of men, who controlled public discourse. Male experience was considered normative. Historically, girls spoke tentatively from outside the dominant male framework. Girls spoke with a different cultural voice, which was produced by the familial and cultural structures of patriarchal power. Usually males more freely and publicly presented experience of self, others, space, and time in objective, individualistic, distant, and authoritative ways. Females generally felt safer in publicly presenting experiences of self in interpersonal, subjective, and immediate ways. (Smith 1987:13)

Women's autobiographies were considered as anomalies-flawed, insignificant, idiosyncratic, or tedious. There was a basic resistance to valuing women's experience. Male autobiographies found a place of privilege, while female autobiographies were devalued and pushed to the margins of the canon. (Smith 1987:16) There was a fundamental distrust and resistance to women's influence, power, and public voice. Although women, in general, were suppressed and repressed, some boldly spoke. They attempted to present their real selves, rather than culturally determined representations.

Late medieval or Renaissance women who were literate and educated found themselves within a new, but limited, world of discourse. There was a new sphere of freedom and opportunity for female, individual expression, but it was within prescribed scripts. Smith contended that there were four basic *life scripts* for women. There was that of the unmarried virgin, the wife, the nun, or the queen. Most women were to remain silent in public. Some women autobiographers wrote letters, diaries, and journals and stayed in their domestic place, out of public discourse, culturally and publicly muted. In some cases, public female autobiographers did not present a true self but a culturally accepted fictitious self or a self revealed in figurative rather than in literal language.

Female writers who had a privileged social status were more likely to write autobiographies in literal language. Others without privileged status often wrote in figurative language (poetry, allegory, myth and so forth). Some female autobiographers dared to confront and negotiate gender ideologies and boundaries in order to publish their stories. Although they were bold enough to enter the world of public discourse, they moved into it from a disadvantaged societal position. Their autobiographies often became *heretic narratives*. (Smith 1987:43) Women's autobiographies were usually seen as illegitimate and contaminating of the genre of autobiography, which has been dominated by male authors. From this perspective, women had no autobiographical selves and no public stories to tell:

> Since the ideology of gender makes of woman's life script a nonstory, a silent space, a gap in patriarchal culture, the ideal woman is self-effacing rather than self-promoting, and her "natural" story shapes itself not around the public, heroic life but around the fluid, circumstantial, contingent responsiveness to others that, according to patriarchal ideology, characterizes the life of woman…(Smith 1987:87)

Effects of Race

The factor of race also affected the content, structure, and style of autobiography, especially as American minorities were, like women, marginalized. Tillie Olsen wrote

"It is an unhappy fact that association with a category: Native-American, Asian-American, *any* hyphenated American, working class, black, women, ethnic, minority, *sub-culture*-U.S.A. American all- has, with occasional exception, relegated a writer to less than full writer's status; resulted as well in ignorance of or lack of full recognition to a writer's work and achievement..." (Olsen, in Tate 1983:x)

Worse than marginalized, African Americans were enslaved. Even after their individual releases before Emancipation, their former slave statuses affected their life stories. They were still not completely free to live and to write about their individual lives. They needed to connect themselves to a corporate identity for the good of their collective culture. Studies of African American, ex-slave narratives revealed a sense of *sameness* about them. With little variance, slave narratives followed a set pattern and structure. They emphasized episodes, which were narrated in a vivid, present-focused, and realistic style. James Olney discussed some of the dynamics of these autobiographies:

"...virtual absence of any reference to memory...but past facts and events of slavery immediately present to the writer and his reader (Thus one often gets, "I can see even now...I can still hear ...")...There is good reason for...rigidly fixed form... The writer of a slave narrative finds himself in an irresolvably tight bind...to give a picture of "slavery *as it is*." (Olney 1984:48)

What were described in the ex-slave narratives were the external realities of slavery, rather than the subjective lives of the narrators. The stories had the same abolitionist motivation. Olney presented the effect of this single purpose:

> The theme is the reality of slavery…the necessity of abolishing it; the content is a series of events…descriptions that…make the reader see…feel the realities of slavery; and form is a chronological, episodic narrative…(Olney 1984:53)

Even after Emancipation and the Civil Rights Movement in the American history, the public lives of female autobiographers of color were especially complex. Smith asserted that, as they suffered double or triple layers of others' misrepresentations and stereotypes, they were all the more marginalized:

> In her doubled, perhaps tripled, marginality, then, the autobiographer negotiates sometimes four sets of stories… written about her rather than by her. Moreover, her non-presence, her unrepresentability, presses even more imperiously yet elusively on her;…her position as speaker before an audience becomes even more precarious. (Smith 1987:51)

Francoise Lionnet contended that Maya Angelou, in the 1970's, directed her autobiography, *I Know Why the Caged Bird Sings*, at white audiences:

> …at the same time it succeeds in gesturing toward the black community, which shares a long tradition among oppressed peoples of understanding duplicitous language for survival. (Lionnet 1989:130)

Lionnet discussed how Angelou addressed the problems of *writing truth* and of *writing for two audiences*. She stated that

Angelou did not reveal her inner self or personal affairs in her book:

> Her narrator alternates between a constative and a performative use of language, simultaneously addressing a white and a black audience, "image making" and instructing, using allegory to talk about history and myths to refer to reality. (Lionnet 1989:131)

Lionnet pointed out the major metaphors of imprisonment and singing which ran through all four of Angelou's autobiographies. She further noted that Angelou's published *struggle* was of a different nature from that of males-more personal and less public or social. (Lionnet 1989:131) She contended that Angelou was cautious, seeking to carefully influence her audience:

> She stages her own alienated relationship to her hypothetical reader, knowing…the reader must be…believing that she has a privileged relation to an autobiographical truth…The double voiced nature of Angelou's text allows her to oppose an oppressive social system without risk of becoming a term within that system, since part of her message…will always elude any direct attempt to inscribe it within the general frame of the dominant discourse. (Lionnet 1989:163)

In an interview with Claudia Tate, Maya Angelou explained her stance of distancing herself in her autobiographies:

> "It's a strange condition, being an autobiographer and a poet. I have to be so internal, and yet while writing, I have to be apart from the story so that I don't fall into indulgence. Whenever I speak about the books, I always think in terms of the Maya character…It's difficult…to preserve this distancing." (Angelou in Tate 1984:3)

Tate further quoted Maya Angelou from an interview with her.

"Protest is a part of my work…I would never get on a soapbox; instead, I would pull in the reader. My work is intended to be slowly absorbed into the system on deeper and deeper levels…" (Angelou in Tate 1984:8)

Tate quoted, from Langston Hughes and Maya Angelou, poetic expressions of the determination and hope for themselves as writers and autobiographers and in general of people of color.

"someday somebody'll
Stand up and talk about me,
And write about me-
and sing about me,
And put on plays about me!
I reckon it'll be
Me myself!" (Langston Hughes, in Tate 1984:xxvi)

"You may write me down in history
With your bitter, twisted lies,
You may trod me in the very dirt
But still, like dust, I'll rise" (Maya Angelou, in Tate 1984:10)

Effects of Performance

In the 1980's and 1990's Spalding Gray produced a unique form of presentation and performance of autobiography. Gray became widely known as an autoperformer. In his monologues Gray appeared as himself and spoke of his personal life: "I am not just a solo performer. I am also an autobiographer that happens to use solo performance as my mode of expression." (letter to

John Gentile 1983:149) Gray presented impressions based on facts, which were outlined but not scripted:

> "I like to think of myself as a…poetic reporter, more like an impressionistic painter than a photographer. Most reporters get the facts out…quickly…fresh news is the best news. I do just the opposite, I give the facts a chance to settle down until…they blend…mix in the swamp of dream, memory and reflection." (Gray 1985:xvi, in Gentile 1989:149)

Although Gray was improvisational and impressionistic in his presentation of his stories, he was still truthful and confessional. (Young 1989:26) He wove personal and social history in what he called *poetic journalism*. Gentile asserted that themes in Gray's performances were particular to him but had universal overtones. He quoted James Leverett:

> It would be false to consider these pieces…narcissistic… unconcerned with such…externals as politics history and society….one of Gray's earliest monologues dealing with his youth…begins and ends with two cataclysmic punctuations: the A-bomb dropped at Hiroshima, the H-bomb at Enewetak. What Gray conveys in between, albeit in the subtlest and most indirect way, is the coming of age in this country after World War II. All of the monologues have had such an added, often hidden, dimension. If you stare at any one of them long enough, you find that what has happened to Gray the world, or least a significant section of it. (Leverett 1985:ix-xiii, in Gentile 1989:149-150)

Conclusion

This historical discussion has provided illustrations of how written and performative autobiographies have been diversely affected by history, culture, social position, gender, race, and performance techniques. Writer and performers of autobiography should take historic, social, and personal contexts into consideration in interpreting autobiographical texts for scriptwriting and performing. They should also realize that autobiographies have been written for many different reasons and purposes.

Scriptwriters/performers should further be aware that there has been great variance in style and form in written and performed autobiographical stories. This has been due in part to the fact that a wide variety of people with varying educational, literary, and artistic backgrounds have been able to write or to perform such work. Written and performative autobiographies have often been simple, common, and free. Frequently, they have been the least literary or theatrical forms of writing or performance. People who have not considered themselves writers or performers have written and performed autobiographical material. (Olney 1980:5)

The artistic or aesthetic gamut of autobiographical production has been broad. Some writers and performers of this genre have had more literary, aesthetic awareness and skill than others have had. Contemporary writers/performers can gain insight from sample historical autobiographies and performances elements that have facilitated marginalization, creativity, and artistry in writing and performing autobiography.

Chapter Two
Lessons from the History of Performance

Introduction

Writers/performers of autobiography can learn valuable lessons about aesthetic elements, dramatic content, and theatrical style from the history of performance. Since many autobiographical performances have been one-person productions, writers/performers of autobiography can gain special insights from the history of solo artistry dating back to ancient performances of poetry, oral storytelling, and singing of tales. Some examples of early one-person performers were the following: rhapsodists, reciters of epic poems in ancient Greece; scops, who composed and sang songs of heroes in Anglo-Saxon England; and jongleurs, who were itinerant minstrels in medieval France.

Every ancient civilization used dramatic performance in some way: in religious ceremonies, funeral rites, and storytelling. Some of the books of the Bible, such as the Song of Songs and the Book of Job, were written in dramatic form. The earliest records of theatrical performances were made in Egypt. One stone tablet was carved 4,000 years ago, depicting the story of a three-day pageant. In this production Ikhernofret arranged and played the leading role. The pageant was made up of actual battles, boat processions, and elaborate ceremonies. Carvings and murals on ancient temple and tomb walls were produced to show highly theatrical pictures of dancing girls and of triumphal processions.

Greek Performance

Greek performance structures and ideas have had tremendous influence throughout history to the present time. In 300 BC, Aristotle identified the significant elements of tragedy as plot, character, thought, diction, music, and spectacle. His classifications have been used in analyzing, writing, and producing drama to the present day. Common, contemporary, Greek theatre terms, such as orchestra, scenery, and proscenium, have been used to the present.

Aspects of Greek theatre structures and the actors' performances in those spaces have persisted in influence. In front of the Acropolis, the theatre of Dionysus was completed in 340 BC. The theater's seats were built into the side of the hill. From that vantage, spectators had a clear view of the *orchestra*, where Dionysus was worshipped with choral dancing and singing. Across the back third of the orchestra was a ten-foot platform, which in time became a stage. Across the rear of this platform (stage) were the decorated fronts of stage buildings, which provided a backdrop and dressing rooms. Greek theatres were roofless. Performances were done in daylight. Changes of scenery were rare. Stage machinery was limited to *thunder machines* and cranes, which lifted actors who represented gods.

Actors wore masks with built-in megaphones to project their voices. They portrayed great legendary figures, wearing heavy, ornamented costumes, high boots, bushy topknots of hair, breast and stomach pads, and trailing robes. (Carlson 1990:65-67) Their costuming caused them to look larger-than-life. In view of the basic, external simplicity of the Greek theatre and staging, performers depended largely on the imagination of the audience and on the writing of the playwright to produce dramatic impact and insight.

Theatrical contests emerged to honor Dionysus, the god of wine and fertility. In 534 Thespis won the first dramatic competition. The term *thespian* (actor) came from his name. (Brockett 1996:60) Patrons defrayed the expenses of staging the competitive plays, and no expense was spared. A director trained the chorus, whose function was to provide objective commentary on the dramatic scenes. A public commissioner supervised the production. First, second, and third monetary prizes were awarded to the playwright/poets for their trilogies. Musicians accompanied the chorus. Music was a fundamental part of Greek education and of the plays. An altar stood in the middle of the orchestra. The Greek world-view included the supernatural and the plays were a part of religious worship.

Aeschylus, Sophocles, and Euripides wrote great Greek tragedies, which are still performed today. Aeschylus introduced dialogue between two characters. Sophocles included a third character in the exchange. He also created dramatic action that led to a definite plot and more realistic, life-like characters. Euripides developed the human-interest element. (Carlson 1990:54-59)

The tragedies revealed conflicts between the will of the gods (often larger-than-life personifications of men characterized by amoral actions) and the ambitions of men. The gods of fate were always more powerful than men, although tragic heroes were portrayed with dignity and courage. (Brockett 1996:74) Usually heroes were confronted with difficult moral choices, struggled with hostile forces, and in the end were defeated (usually in death). Greek tragedies were dramatically complex. They dealt with significant ethical problems, which the protagonists struggled to solve for the good of the aristocratic society. The tragic plays were designed to purge the spectator's soul through the emotions of fear and pity. They were also designed to help the spectators accept the challenges in their own lives by seeing the characters in the plays experience far worse difficulties. Leading characters commonly met their demise due to tragic flaws, which were excesses of otherwise good virtues.

Tragedy on stage declined after 400 BC, but Greek comedy was alive. It was more natural in vocal delivery and more energetic in movement. However, it was dominantly bawdy, obscene, and farcical. Aristophanes developed *Old Comedy,* which was satirical of political and social issues. *New Comedy*, which followed*,* emphasized domestic, situational, private, and personal intrigues. (Carlson 1990:64)

Elements of Greek drama continue to provide instructive models for effective theater performances today. Greek tragedies recounted stories, which traced the cycle of death to life. They encouraged an acceptance of the difficult and even tragic events of life. Violence was not portrayed on stage. Rather, it happened off stage and was reported by messengers. The protagonists were larger-than-life characters who struggled with universal issues. Their tragic flaws were often subtle excesses of good virtues. Greek performances incorporated elements of music and poetry. Classification of dramatic elements facilitated analysis and interpretation of the plays.

The development of Greek drama from tragedies, to political comedy, to domestic or situational comedy is instructive. A gradual downward spiral developed, to be repeated later in dramatic history. This was marked by the decline of the religious and philosophical nature of the dramas to that which became increasingly coarse and more entertainment-oriented.

Roman Performance

Roman drama copied and imitated Greek drama. Although Roman versions in Latin later influenced Shakespeare and other playwrights, Roman imitations of Greek drama were inferior. More popular than plays in Rome were the spectacles of chariot races, gladiator battles, and fights with wild animals. Romans, in general, did not seem interested in performances that provoked thoughtful reaction. They seemed more interested in theatre that would entertain, arouse passions, and thrill. As the empire wound down (destroyed from within), Roman life, in general, became more decadent. Romans became increasingly involved with sensuality and violence. During much of the history of the Roman Empire, audiences were entertained by violent, bloody, and obscene spectacle. Eroticism became more excessive. Exaggerated sexuality began to adorn architecture, as in Pompeii. Creativity decreased in the arts. Music even became more bombastic. (Schaeffer 1984:26) Constantine, a Christian Roman emperor, put a stop to bloody spectacles in the Roman coliseums. As the Church came to power in Rome, much of the decadent Roman entertainment was stopped.

Some Roman dramatic techniques in plays did survive, however. Seneca's techniques of the five-act form, use of elaborate and flowery language, themes of retaliation and revenge, magic rites and ghosts, and the device of the confidante or trusted friend, influenced later playwrights. Elements of adaptations of Greek *New Comedy* by Plautus and Terence survived to influence later works. (Crawford 1995:120) Some of these tropes were mistaken identities, free-spending sons, deceiving fathers, and humorous intrigues among slaves (later among servants). Pantomime was also evident in Roman entertainment and has survived until today. In the Roman culture, words were written for the ear in public oratory. (Pelias 1992:32)

Medieval Performance

During the Middle Ages most plays were religiously oriented. They portrayed Bible stories or conveyed church doctrine. The language of the Bible and of the church was Latin, not the common vernacular of the people. Thus, the people were dependent on the priests to teach them the Bible and church doctrine. Drama became an instructional tool in the hands of priests and choirboys to teach biblical stories and lessons of the church. Passion plays depicting the life of Christ were produced in chancels, which were at the front of the churches. Plays depicting the lives of saints were produced in naves, which were in the main interior of churches, closer to audiences. Then *cycle plays* were performed on outdoor stages at the entrances of churches for viewing by outside audiences. (Carlson 1990:118)

The typical stage upon which these plays were performed was a plain wooden platform. At one end were the pearly gates of Heaven and at the other were the flaming jaws of Hell. (Brockett 1996:91) At the conclusion of the play the good characters went into the gates of Heaven and the bad characters went into the gates of Hell. In time this stage was put on wheels to be made moveable. Thus, the first pageants and pageant wagons were created. The word "pageant" meant "rolling platform." Guilds produced cycle pageant plays. In the hands of laymen, however, imaginative material was added. For example, Noah had great difficulty persuading his wife to come along in the cycle version of the story of Noah. Having put her aboard the ark, he came forward to urge the men in the audience to take their wives in hand early in their married life. Noah's wife came forward, as well, to warn the ladies that if they were wise, they would not marry at all.

The plays on pageant wagons drew great crowds. In some cases innkeepers saw this as a chance for business. Actors with these pageant wagons were probably enticed with food, drink, and lodging, if they would perform their plays in the courtyards of inns. However, the audiences in these environments would have been primarily interested in entertainment and in hilarity. Earlier audiences, who had come to the entrances of churches to see religious plays, came more out of reverence, worship, and desire to learn biblical truths. The audiences of plays on pageant wagons were often more entertained by the characters who went into the flaming gates of Hell than those who were righteous and went to Heaven. The players, who had freedom with changing and improvising their lines, began to accommodate to the entertainment interests of audiences. There was a gradual downward spiral in the presentation of great biblical characters, from models for religious education to performances of these characters as buffoons for amusement.

Drama in the Middle Ages degenerated from an educational tool of the church to more of a vehicle for merriment. An historic pattern seems to have been repeated. Greek drama had declined from religious plays with great universal themes to amusing productions with more domestic, crude, situational comedy. Similarly, the religious drama of the Middle Ages declined to more coarse entertainment. The emphasis on theatre productions as forms of religious worship, teaching, and inspiration shifted to an emphasis on dramatic performance for entertainment and amusement.

The Dark Ages were not totally dark, however, in performance history. Simple, aesthetic performances were common in the forms of mime, improvisations, and storytelling accompanied by music. Bible stories were recounted through drama. However, aesthetic deterioration was facilitated, when performances were given in environments where rowdy, sometimes drunken audiences reinforced coarse, comic elements.

Reformation and Renaissance Performance

The Reformation reacted to, stood against, and changed much of the religious distortion and degeneration of the Middle Ages. In 1643 Puritans closed the doors of theatres because they subverted, in their opinion, public morals. However, the arts, especially music and visual arts flourished in northern Europe within biblical boundaries and within the Christian concept of reality. During the Reformation and Renaissance, natural and realistic art replaced that which was mystical and symbolic. In Reformation countries, art was produced for the glory of God, who was at the center of the universe for Reformation man. (Schaeffer 1984:79-88)

As the Reformation took place in northern Europe, the Renaissance took place in southern Europe. In Renaissance countries, art was produced which glorified man, who was at the center of the universe for Renaissance thinkers. The Renaissance was generally humanistic in orientation with little reference to absolutes, universals, or a unified concept of ultimate truth. Thomas Aquinas, as a Renaissance forerunner, had opened the door to the exalting of the human mind and to individual relativism, when he stated that man's will had succumbed to the Fall but not his mind. There was a return to the classical Greek philosophers, who were to stand beside the great biblical figures, including the apostles. For example, Michelangelo's David was created with larger-than-life hands and body. This

David was not circumcised, indicating that he was a humanistic David (not necessarily the David of the Bible). Great art flourished in the Renaissance but morality in art gradually declined. Mary, for example, was painted as a real figure, but the king's mistress was used as a model. (Schaeffer 1984:71-72)

Great dramatic literature flourished under the patronage of Queen Elizabeth. Earlier religious plays were replaced with the sweeping histories, tragedies, and comedies of Shakespeare and of other great Elizabethan playwrights. Actors were respected members of society during the reign of Elizabeth. They often traveled with repertory companies and played a variety of roles. (Brockett 1996:105-106) Acting was more natural but the roles of women were still played by boys. Actors' performances were open and presentational to audiences in Elizabethan theatres, which were of simple design. Actors performed to highly involved audiences. Members of the audience were close to the stage in the *yard* into which the elevated platform projected. This yard was in a large, unroofed area, which was enclosed by a three-storied gallery.

William Shakespeare wrote in blank verse during this period. He followed Thomas Kyd, who had established this writing style as a hallmark of the period in *The Spanish Tragedy*. Shakespeare also borrowed from earlier fiction, histories, myths, and playwriting techniques. He contributed few new playwriting elements, but he brought them to greater aesthetic heights. Like the Greeks, he wrote about great philosophical issues, probed to the depths the complexities of his characters, and portrayed human emotion with intensity.

Shakespeare's theater, the Globe, was situated across the Thames from London, on the "wrong side" of the river. Queen Elizabeth conceived this compromise arrangement to pacify the Puritans. The Globe was a simple, open roofed, circular, wooden, tiered theater. Staging was simple. Shakespeare's dramatic literature was rich in aesthetic elements and characterizations. Performances were energetic and intense. Members of all strata of society were represented in Shakespearean plays, and they related to all classes of people. (Brockett 1996:108-112) However, many of his plays, like those of other playwrights of his time, included coarse elements for popular appeal.

Seventeenth Century Performance

In the seventeenth century, comedy again became the dominant dramatic form. Women appeared on the stage for the first time. Unfortunately, these women tended to be the mistresses of the male actors and were often viewed as sexual objects. Actors wore extravagant costumes. Likewise, the set and stage effects were elaborate. A proscenium arch was used to frame the stage and within it scenery was changed. Situational comedy was the dominant dramatic form. *Comedy of Manners* made fun of the upper classes' attitudes and moralities. The acting voice was elevated and movement was carefully executed. (Crawford 1995:187)

Racine and Corneille turned to the Greeks as models for their tragedies. Moliere produced great comedies. The characters of Moliere were more psychologically complex than characters of English Restoration, gentlemen playwrights. Restoration characters were more one-dimensional. Restoration comedy primarily involved witticisms, repartee, and risqué intrigues for comic entertainment. The Restoration theatre provided a seated pit, galleries, and boxes for its aristocratic audiences. It incorporated wings off the stage, a system of flat painted scenery, and an entirely roofed-in theatre. A managerial system of non-theatre people emerged. (Carlson 1990:232-246)

The development in English theatre history from great Elizabethan drama with complex, universal characters to seventeenth century, domestic comedy with one-dimensional characters is reflective of earlier downward dramatic declines, as in Greek and medieval dramatic history. The pattern of the development of great, didactic, religious, and tragic drama to situational comedy was repeated. There was again a downward moral, aesthetic spiral in dramatic content and style, especially in England. Powerful complex Elizabethan plays declined to Restoration situational comedies, which were more simplistic in dramatic nature even though they were staged elaborately.

Eighteenth Century Performance

During the Enlightenment, Reason was exalted. The middle classes were on the rise and so was social consciousness. Man was considered perfectible by his reason. In theatre a pseudo-sophisticated attitude was evident. Neo-classical ideas, such as those concerned with unities of time, space, and action, overly constrained plays. There was a general focus on logic, rationality, reason, and control. It was also a period of revolution. France experienced the Reign of Terror during the French Revolution. Peace came later at the price of the dictatorship of Napoleon. In France, where individual human reason was the primary authority, there was not a general belief in universal absolutes. (Schaeffer 1984:120-122) In the United States the American Revolution ended with the writing of the Constitution, which was guided by biblical principles and based on a belief in absolute Lex Rex (law above the king). It established American representative government.

Since performance opportunities were limited for English actors, who were not attached to one of the two London theatres licensed by the king, one-man "entertainments" were devised to circumvent and to provide relief from theatrical restrictions imposed since the Restoration. Samuel Foote (1721-1777), a British satirist and failed tragedian, seems to have originated one-man burlesques. He was skillful at mimicking well-known actors of the day. George Alexander Stevens (1710-1784), who performed with actor/manager David Garrick, was popular as a one-man burlesque presenter and monologist. In his satirical lectures, Stevens poked fun at famous people and at social stereotypes. Thus, one-person performances flourished in England in the eighteenth century. (Young 1989:13-16)

Nineteenth Century Performance

The emphasis on reason shifted in the nineteenth century to a dominating, romantic appeal to man's emotions. There was a fascination with gothic, supernatural, fantastical, and eerie themes. Self-expression was emphasized. Beethoven produced in this stream. So did poets such as Wordsworth and Coleridge. Rosseau encouraged autonomous freedom and a return to the concept of the *noble savage*. He promoted a return to nature. He believed it was society that corrupted man. Leading artists who tried to live according to this Bohemian ideal, however, despaired in the end. Gauguin, who went to Tahiti to find and to paint the *noble savage* died in desperation, as did many of his impressionistic artist friends. (Schaeffer 1984:158-159)

Plays were loosely concerned with facts, but more with emotional extremes. Plots were contrived and dealt more with an imaginary world. Romantic actors were frequently melodramatic and flamboyant. Charles Matthews distinguished himself in the early nineteenth century as a mimic, comedian, and one-person performer. (Young 1989:17) One-person performances received unprecedented popular support in the United States during the second half of the nineteenth century. This was the "golden age of platform performances." (Gentile 1989:xvii-24)

Several factors contributed to the popularity of one-person platform performances. First, they were considered commercially viable. Secondly, during the Victorian Age, there was a strong clerical resistance to the theater. This was somewhat justified as prostitutes frequented the *third tier* to meet clientele. The platform with its lectures and solo readings of literature was considered genteel, dignified, respectable, and edifying. Thus, it was able to draw broad popular and mainline support. After the American Civil War, the demand for non-theatre entertainment was strong. There was widespread literacy and interest in hearing the written word read or recited. The travel needs of solo performers were provided by railroads. (Gentile 1989:1-6)

One of the most popular performers in Britain and in the United States was Charles Dickens. He was adored by the public, more like a popular star would be today. His was the greatest one-man show of the nineteenth century. (Fitzsimmons 1970:15,in Gentile 1989:11) He had aspired to be an actor in his youth. He performed characters from his writings, breaking from the elocutionary style of the day. He characterized his presentations as popular entertainments. Paul Schlicke wrote, "Direct appeal was of the essence in his public readings." (Schlicke 1985:230,in Gentile 1989:15) His daughter, Mamie, wrote that he threw "himself completely into the character he was creating and…had become in action, as in imagination the character of his pen." (Dickens n.d.:48,in Gentile 1989:15) He was wonderfully expressive with his body and face, performing with energetic character gestures. His reviews were mixed, however. It was said by some that he succeeded in dialogue more than in recitation, as he was more of an animated storyteller than he was a reader.

In the nineteenth century platform lectures or performances were common. *Lyceum* bureaus, which were usually paid a ten per cent commission, served as booking agencies for lecturers and contracting parties. Notable American and English figures spoke on American platforms during this period. Among the most celebrated were Daniel Webster, Ralph Waldo Emerson, Henry David Thoreau, Alexander Graham Bell, and Oliver Wendell Holmes. Distinguished authors publicized their writing and secured supplemental income by platform presentations. (Gentile 1989:19)

During the nineteenth century, as Charles Dickens was distinguished for his character performances, Edgar Allen Poe was noted for his performances of poetry. During the American Civil War, James Murdock, a popular Shakespearean actor, served his country with benefit readings, designed to arouse patriotic spirit. Murdoch displayed great virtuosity and craft as an elocutionist. A reviewer described him in the *New York Leader*:

> "Mr. Murdoch…is a magnificent elocutionist, and reads
> not only with mechanical skill, and an intellectual
> appreciation of the subject, but with an intense feeling
> that arouses a corresponding emotion in his audience.
> Every shade of meaning, every subtlety of passion that the
> text suggests, is conveyed in his changing intonations…"
> (Bowyer 1952:65, in Gentile 1989:23)

Anna Cora Mowatt, Fanny Kemble, and Charlotte Cushman were also popular platform performers in the mid-nineteenth century. They brought prestige to their art, securing respectability and acceptance for female solo artists, who would follow them. Mowatt, who performed material from major and minor poets, received excellent reviews in New York newspapers. Henry Wadsworth Longfellow and Henry James praised Fanny Kemble's platform readings of Shakespeare. (Gentile 1989:24-34) Emma Stebbins praised Charlotte Cushman:

"She seemed to cast off…every suggestion of any other life but the one she was for the time to interpret. She identified herself with it…she…seemed to gather in all her audience and hold them, as it were, by a…spell of potent and irresistible magnetism,-she set aside all feeling of personal identity, and lived, and moved, and acted the varied personages…they lived before us…" (Stebbins 1878:91,in Gentile 1989:35)

At the end of Charlotte Cushman's career as a platform performer, the Chautauqua Assembly was founded. Chautauqua gatherings primarily began as Sunday-school meetings held in the woods for lectures, lessons, sermons, devotions, and conferences. People who attended the camp-like meetings were housed in tents. The first two-week course was held on the shores of Chautauqua Lake in New York. What began primarily for religious instruction was broadly expanded for cultural education at various sites. Fifteen years after the first course at Lake Chautauqua, there were one hundred independent assemblies across the United States. Lyceum presentations were conducted in comfortable auditoriums in the winter, but Chautauqua meetings were held outdoors in the summer. Famous performers, seen on both circuits, were Robert McLean Cumnock, Helen Potter, and Leland Powers. Robert McLean Cumnock, who excelled at interpreting Dickens and Scottish literature, was a teacher of elocution at Northwestern University. Helen Potter was known as a credible impersonator of notable female actors and lecturers. She portrayed Susan B. Anthony, Sarah Berhardt, Charlotte Cushman, Fanny Kemble, and Elizabeth Cady Statton. She also depicted national, male figures such as Edwin Booth and Abraham Lincoln. Reviews provided commentary on her depth and range of performance. Leland Powers appeared simply in evening clothes to portray a host of characters. Pearson described Powers as, "The first to present modern plays as monologues, Mr. Powers has the ability, and the genius…to keep him always in the lead of the many others who present the same art form." (Pearson 1908:15,in Gentile 1989:46)

Chautauqua presentations were originally considered more respectable than other types of popular entertainment, such as vaudeville shows. Vaudeville had developed from minstrel and variety productions and had become increasing popular. Around the turn of the century, Chautuaqua and lyceum performances, which originally appealed to the gentry, became more entertaining. Vaudeville entertainment, which originally appealed to the masses, became more respectable.

During the last decade of the century, a remarkable personality appeared on platforms. It was Samuel Clemens as Mark Twain, the popular American humorist and master storyteller. John Gentile described him as "the best of the American writer-performers as well as the finest platform humorist of his age." Using relaxed, colloquial language, Twain performed with the impression of improvised, momentary, impulses, which he described as "studied fictions."

"Fictitious heresies for the right word, fictitious
unconscious pauses, fictitious unconscious side remarks,
fictitious unconscious embarrassments, fictitious unconscious
emphases placed on the wrong word with a deep intention back of
these and all the other artful fictive shades which give
to a recited tale the captivating naturalness of an
impromptu narration…" (Clemens 1959:181,in Gentile 1989:57)

The turn of the century was marked by great platform
performances of literary dramatic monologues. Solo performers
were prolific at this time. They described themselves as
elocutionists, readers, reciters, characterists, impersonators,
monologists, storytellers, and expressionists. This development
reflected a romantic interest in the individual. It was a rich
period for one-person performances of great literature and of
fascinating characters.

Twentieth Century Performance

At the turn of the twentieth century, stage plays were
often marked by the development of realism and then naturalism
with sad or tragic themes. New experimental theater forms
emerged after WWI, which were commonly marked by chance,
fragmentation, and hopelessness. There was little appeal to
reason and logic, but rather to non-reason and non-rationality.

On the other hand, twentieth-century, one-person
performances were more frequently characterized by positive,
redemptive, and celebratory elements. Early in the century,
platform performance developed into solo theatre, after the
decline of Tent Chautauqua and Lyceum Circuits. An outstanding
solo performer in the early twentieth century was Ruth Draper.
She was a multilingual character actress. Convinced that if she

believed in what she was performing the audience would believe it, Ruth Draper broke all records for solo performances in her vast array of characterizations for the New York Comedy Theater's 1928-29 season. Jordan Young wrote that Draper portrayed

> …beggars and society ladies with equal credibility. From starving waif to giddy debutante, Balkan peasant to French dressmaker, her characterizations were true to life. Her Scottish immigrant at Ellis Island was no less authentic than her temperamental Polish actress or her New York matron at an Italian lesson, or her portrait of a rural Irish woman recalling the death of her only son. (Young 1989:37)

Young noted the simplicity in Draper's productions:

> She accomplished her magic with the slightest of costumes
> and the simplest of props- a shawl, an occasional
> hat or cloak, a handbag or an umbrella. The stage was
> adorned by no more than a chair or table; it was often
> bare of all furniture. (Young 1989:37-38)

Draper explained her approach to an interviewer:

> It is the audience who must supply the imagination…
> What is really important is…to bring the audience up onto
> the stage and into the scene with you. It is they who
> must give you even more than you give them in the way
> of imagination and creative power. (Young 1989:38)

Ruth Draper was popular with common people and government leaders in the United States and in Great Britain for nearly three decades. Other popular performers from 1920-1950 were Cissie Loftus, Dorothy Sands, and Charles Laughton. Particularly notable was Cornelia Otis Skinner in her performances of the multiple *Wives of Henry VIII* and three generations of women in *Edna His Wife*, which was a full-length adaptation of a best-selling novel.

After WWII some American playwrights developed psychologically realistic plays with penetrating analyses of human characters in simplified settings and in compressed time. However, sadness, tragedy, cynicism, pessimism, and/or hopelessness often pervaded these plays. New theater forms emerged after WWII, which were often marked by desire for escapism. After WWII Theater of the Absurd became influential. Since Absurdists thought there was little hope in reason or in the emotions, they tended to emphasize the illogical, confusing, and hostile elements in life. Their plays put strange people, in strange episodes, in strange relationships. In this vein were Samuel Beckett's *Waiting for Godot* and Edward Albee's *Zoo Story*. (Carlson 1990:524-530) For modern, twentieth-century, humanistic man, there was commonly little reference to universal absolutes. For many there was little hope except in existentialism and non-reason.

A refreshing renaissance in one-person shows emerged in the 1950's and 1960's. Emlyn Williams portrayed Charles Dickens. Hal Holbrook presented Mark Twain. One-person biographical shows were prolific in the 1970's and 1980's. Julie Harris portrayed Emily Dickinson and Charlotte Bronte; James Whitmore, Theodore Roosevelt, Harry Truman, and Will Rogers; Alec McCowen, Rudyard Kipling; Henry Fonda, Clarence Darrow; Ben Kingsley, Edmund Kean; and James Earl Jones, Paul Robeson and so forth.

In the 1980's one-person performances of Shakespeare and the Bible emerged. John Gielgud performed the *Ages of Man*.

Ian McKellen presented *Acting Shakespeare*. Alec McCowen presented *St. Mark's Gospel*. Ben Kingsley won an Oscar for his film portrayal of Gandhi. Lily Tomlin, Whoopi Goldberg, and Eric Bogosian were famed monologists. Dylan Thomas was popular as a writer/performer.

In the 1980's, performers of *biography* presented their characters impressionistically. A resistance to character duplication, replication, or reproduction developed. Many notable performers sought to subtly reveal their character's subjective experience through suggestion. Julie Harris said of Emily Dickinson in *The Belle of Amherst,* "This is not a literal life of the poet. We tried to capture her mystique." (Wahls 1976:4,in Gentile 1989:144))

There was a performance shift from *biography* to *subjective autobiography* and to *autoperformance*. In the 1980's-1990's, Spalding Gray captivated audiences with *autoperformative* storytelling. He was followed by other autobiographical monologists, who performed in a storytelling style similar to that of Gray. In 1995, Lynn Miller and Jacqueline Taylor wrote the editorial preface of "Performing Autobiography," in *Text and Performance Quarterly*. They stated, "…the study of autobiography has increasingly occupied performance studies scholars…solo performance of autobiographical narratives has become as commonplace as performances showcasing literary works created by others…twenty years ago." (Miller & Taylor 1995:v)

In the 1990's, Anna Deveare Smith promoted social awareness and facilitated social understanding, as she remarkably performed a host of African American and Jewish individuals in her one-woman show, *Fires in the Mirror*. Concerned with individual voices within conflicting racial groups, Smith immersed herself in the inner-city, minority cultures in Crown Heights in Brooklyn, New York. Her intervention involved listening to and then performing individuals, who normally would not be heard, from the conflicting, racial groups. She conducted lengthy personal interviews of key individuals from the Black and Jewish communities. These individuals had been involved with the tragic death of a young African American boy. The boy was playing on a sidewalk, when the car of a rabbi went over the curb and killed the child. This incident touched off intense racial hostilities.

Smith transcribed with great precision the voices of those she interviewed. She established the identity of those she performed by listening to, transcribing, and replicating their speech. She then mirrored many of these individuals as she portrayed them. Through *Fires in the Mirror*, she performed individuals from both groups by using their own words. (Reinelt 1996:609-617) She used the process she developed in Crown Heights in Los Angles following the Rodney King verdict to produce her one-woman production, *Twilight*. She built bridges of understanding. Her research and subsequent powerful performances were novel. Her approach was others-based. Her research and performances brought compassionate insight into racial tensions in inner cities.

In the 1990's, performance of oneself as autobiographical performance was often connected with *performance art*. Male artists in the 1960's had largely begun the development of the theory and practice of performance art, as they sought a simplified, artistic performance of physical bodies in space. From the 1970's to the 1990's, feminist performance artists expanded the originally visual, image-based art to word-based art, which was concerned primarily with text and narrative. Feminist performers were less concerned with abstract performance art than with performance art, which concerned real, specific, social, and political issues. The significant questions of these feminist, autobiographical performers were concerned with a woman's place in society. In autobiographical performances, feminist artists frequently performed events from personal history in exploration of self-discovery and in celebration of self-empowerment, in such ways as to produce forums in which they were able to reach out to other women with experiences like their own.

Feminist autobiographical performers frequently presented multiple personae or identities. In the late 1990's, feminist performers of autobiography seemed to be re-thinking self-representation as not only individual but grounded in particular cultures, in specific communities, in race, in class, and in gender. They were concerned with providing a voice for hitherto silenced and suppressed groups. (Carlson 1996:600-605)

In their performances, there was sometimes a blend between fact and fiction as they revealed themselves. Editors Leslie Satin and Judith Jerome of *Women & Performance, a Journal of Feminist Theory*, during the summer of 1999, in the issue "Performing Autobiography," wrote that "autobiography is a telling of the self that develops over time, that is invented and reinvented, that changes shape and character no matter how solid its worldly 'facts.'" (Satin & Jerome 1999:11). In 1996, Marvin Carlson, in *Modern Drama*'s issue "Autobiographical Performance," discussed the continuum, which included material from everyday life and reconstructions of autobiographical performance and the constructions of narrative and narrator in feminist autobiographical performance:

> …It would…be…difficult to construct a clear line between
> …"characters" of traditional drama and the authentic
> "alternate identities" of autobiographical performance.
> It is probably safer to think of a continuum stretching

from the performance of actual autobiographical material through improvised autobiographical fantasies…to scripted multiple identities…to enacted characters…to familiar tradition of stage monologues…to characters in conventional plays…slippage…operates…as processes of selection and narrativity operate…the same sort of distance that inevitably exists between the actual life experience… and the autobiographical structuring of it, necessarily exists also between the I that lived that experience and the I that narrates it to an audience. Both narrative and narrator are constructions. The role the actor now plays is a role which she claims as her own, but it remains a role, still deeply involved in both mimesis and representation. (Carlson 1996:603-604)

Carlson continued, in his 1996 article "Performing Self," to discuss the struggle of feminist performers of autobiography with their awareness of how self is constructed in codes in marginalized groups:

Some such codes operated on the level of the organization of the material - codes of selection, of narration, of representation, of performance- while others operated at the level of the material itself - involving all sorts of cultural assumptions…In short, the "identity" articulated by autobiographical performance was discovered to be already a role, character, following scripts not controlled by the performer but by the culture…(Carlson 1996:604)

In the late 1990's, autobiographical performers were more self-reflexive in light of heightened awareness of issues of identity in social, cultural, and political life and due to the desire to give voice to marginalized groups. First, feminist autobiographical performers, then performers from other marginalized groups, in the late 1990's, sought to establish specific, authentic identities and to disengage themselves from false identities constructed for them by the dominant culture. Further, it seems autobiographical performance artists as members of marginalized groups sought specific, true identities in order to effectively position themselves for social and political activism. They seemed to believe that intervention in dominant psychological, linguistic, social, cultural, political, theatrical, and performative systems required truthful identity positions and representations, even if they were in progress or flexible. These flexible representations presented changing selves or multiple roles, sides, or facets of self. Carlson wrapped up his analysis of the autobiographical performance history of the 1970's-1990's, in "Autobiographical Performance," by writing:

> ...the enactment of autobiography itself, like the enactment of autobiographical fantasy, has come back around to converge with mimesis, distinguished from conventional theatre less by the operations of enactment than by the reliance upon a solo performer portraying a variety of constructed personae…This fascination with the margins, with ambiguity, with double-codings can be seen everywhere in contemporary art…Performance art has pressed us not only to acknowledge that character, role, and identity are far more fluid categories, but also to use this acknowledgement…for increasing the richness of our theatre experience, of our awareness of ourselves, and of our culture. (Carlson 1996:606-607)

The twentieth century was filled with creative and fascinating performance experimentation. Marked by significant social activism, twentieth century performance promoted awareness of the need for truthful identity in marginalized groups who had struggled to free themselves of imposed, stereotypical, and/or false identities imposed by dominant cultural groups. Diversity in performance was encouraged. University performance studies departments expanded theater, dance, literature and other related studies to include performance issues from cultures around the world. Multi-media technologies enriched visual and auditory production elements. Video, computer, television, and film technologies facilitated access to performances. American and international musical theatre richly developed. Theater pieces, which expounded biblical truth and which provided hope, emerged. Revivals of romantic, classic tales and early American musicals provided refreshment in an era often characterized by escapism and non-reason (reflected even in Seinfeld's situational comedy-about nothing).

It was also an age of post-modern thinking commonly characterized by little belief in absolutes or universals. Ambiguity and uncertainty was often dominant. It was a century commonly marked by pessimism, cynicism, and hope only in existentialism. In the twentieth century, the comic-tragedy genre developed; laughter was stimulated by slapstick activities of pathetic people in pathetic situations. Almost anything was accepted for comic relief. Often visual spectacle superceded substance in performance. Drama became increasingly coarse, erotic, and violent. At the end of the twentieth century, artistic performances frequently reflected elements at the bottom of the downward aesthetic spiral, which were evident in earlier periods of dramatic history.

Conclusion

Throughout the history of performance, one-person performances took an array of shapes. There were readings, recitations, impersonations, monologues, performances of transcriptions, adaptations, and biographies. Most recently, new forms such as autoperformances, performance art, and subjective autobiographies have been performed with an emphasis on self-identity and/or multiple identities. It is instructive to note some of the elements, which have strengthened enduring, autobiographical stories, rendering them classics.

Central to good stories are intriguing and colorful characters. If an autobiographical writer/performer chooses a character displaying a fascinating personality and an engaging use of language, he or she is more insured of an aesthetic, impacting, and easily produced script and performance. Performer Leia Morning, a scholar of American and British literature, who portrays Virginia Woolf, Jane Austen, and Charlotte Bronte, states, "In a way, it's not acting...It's like really being someone else and allowing the genius of that person to operate through you." (Young 1989:33)

Classic stories, which survive the test of time from generation to generation, seem to be about characters who are larger-than-life and whose lives reflect universal issues. These characters often overcome significant physical, personal, social, or cultural barriers. Having complex, multi-dimensional personalities, they are often paradoxical. They are usually intense, passionate, or energetic. They are frequently unique, colorful, reflective, and insightful. Through their responses to life events, they commonly teach and inspire. As they develop over time, they are often role models.

Part II

Choosing and Studying
the Character

**Carlotta Russell Maneice
as Sojourner Truth**

Chapter Three
Role Modeling

Introduction

Writers/performers should consider, in choosing a character to present, the potential role modeling effect of autobiographies. This literary and performative genre focuses on the internal, subjective realities, struggles, development, or growth of characters. Autobiographical writing/performing can present characters as role models in their struggles to answer questions about themselves or others, to make significant decisions, to overcome personal or cultural barriers, to contribute to society, and so forth. Evidence supports the idea that performing autobiography may provide a role modeling effect, which may influence achievement motivation in audiences. This role modeling effect may be particularly significant in marginalized groups such as women and minorities.

This text provides evidence of the power of role models to significantly affect achievement motivation in observers. The studies presented in this chapter directly and indirectly relate to the power of role models, presented through writing and performing autobiography, to affect achievement motivation in audiences. The author is conducting research with her college, performance studies, communication students, which concerns the significance of role modeling through writing and performing autobiography. Further, she encourages others who use this text to conduct related research and replication of the studies discussed in this chapter.

In 1996, the author provided evidence that the variable of *locus of control,* which is considered a reliable and valid construct and predictor of achievement, could be affected and changed by the identification of role models in female college students. Further, she presented evidence, which supported the idea that female college students who identified role models had stronger internal locus of control than did those who did not identify role models. (Howard, 1996)

The author is currently expanding, with her students and alumni, the investigation of the relationship between role models and locus of control (defined more fully in this chapter). This current research is studying the relationship between role modeling through videoconference performances of African American autobiographies and locus of control in college audience members. These audience members are students in a long-distance, African American history program and are mostly African Americans themselves.

Evidence Related to Cognitive and Social Learning Theories

In recent decades, cognitive learning theories have developed, which have focused on achievement motivation in terms of attributions and observations. Rotter has contributed to cognitive theories of recent decades with his social learning theory, a social-personality theory that describes individuals in terms of their tendencies to attribute success or failure to internal or external factors. He wrote

…the extent to which a person believes that he can control what happens to him is referred to as a belief in internal control of reinforcement. A belief that one is controlled by luck, fate, or others, is referred to as a belief in external control of reinforcement. (Rotter 1971:61)

Weiner, likewise, has provided a systematic achievement motivation theory, which begins with the assumption that students *attribute* their successes and failures to internal or external causes. Those who attribute their successes to internal causes seem to have a greater degree of achievement motivation than those who attribute their successes to external causes. (Weiner, 1979)

One facet of research regarding locus of control concerns how it affects people's perceptions of themselves. Locus of control seems to affect people's perception of rewards they receive as being controlled by internal factors, such as their personal ability, effort, or skill, or as controlled by external factors, such as chance, luck, or other people. Peoples' perceptions of their environments as determined by skill or chance seems to influence positive or negative shifts of achievement expectancy. In addition, there are other characteristics that have emerged as a result of individuals' perceptions of their environments as personally or externally controlled. For example, research investigations suggest that people classified as internal in locus of control display more information-seeking behavior and make better use of this information than people classified as external in locus of control. (Weiner 1979:272)

Related investigations have been especially important for females. The author has presented evidence that suggests the following:

- Female subjects who identify female role models have stronger internal locus of control than female subjects who do not identify female role models.
- Locus of control in female subjects is a changeable variable.
- Internal locus of control in female subjects increases over the first year of college in those who have female role models.
- Internal locus of control decreases over the first year of college in female students who do not have female role models.

Thus, the author's findings suggest a factor, which may strengthen internal locus of control in first-year, female, coeducational, college students and therefore may strengthen their achievement motivation. (Howard 1996:vii-viii)

Evidence Related to Observation and Achievement Theories

Cognitive and social learning theories have included the issue of learning by observation. Bandura asserted, "Most human behavior is learned observationally through modeling: from observing others one forms an idea of how new behaviors are performed…Models who possess engaging qualities are sought out…" (Bandura 1977:22-23)

Evidence exists related to the question of the relationship of internal locus of control and role models in coeducational, college settings. Strengthening the internal locus of control in students seems to be related to improving achievement of students and seems to point towards a solution for female and minority under-achievement and under-representation. (Howard 1996:6-14) Achievement theory includes "expectancy value," which describes how hard one works at achievement as determined by one's expectancy of success and his/her valuing of that success. Achievement motivation involves determination to accomplish something difficult; to organize; or to master objects, people, or ideas. (Weiner, 1979) In Weiner's theory of motivation, "individuals classified as high versus low in achievement needs exhibit opposing risk preferences when given tasks differing in perceived difficulty…persons labeled high in achievement needs are predicted to exhibit different risk-taking behavior than persons low in achievement needs." (Weiner 1986:10)

Locus of Control

Locus of control identifies the extent to which persons perceive that events in their lives are contingent upon their own behavior or own characteristics. (Rotter, 1966) Locus of control may be operationally measured by Rotter's Internal-External Locus of Control Scale. (Rotter, 1966) Persons with internal locus of control believe they have control over reinforcing events in their lives. (Stone & Jackson, 1975) Individuals with internal locus of control attribute change to their actions. They believe and act as though they control their own futures and see themselves as effective in determining the occurrence of reinforcing events. (Stone & Jackson, 1975) People with external locus of control attribute change to external sources. They believe, report, or act as though forces beyond their control (such as fate, chance, powerful others, social constraints, or instructions) are important factors in determining the occurrence of reinforcing events. (Stone & Jackson, 1975) Persons with external locus of control perceive that reinforcement follows some action of their own but is not entirely contingent upon their action. They believe that reinforcement is "the result of luck, chance, fate, as under the control of powerful others, or is unpredictable because of the great complexity of the forces." (Rotter 1966:227)

Role Model

A role model is an adult who has qualities or skills that a person "...admires and wishes to emulate... The process of observing can take place without direct interaction between the observer and the role model. It is possible that the role model may not be aware of his or her...influence on another person."
(Anderson & Ramsey 1990:183)

Role models in social learning theory have been defined as examples to imitate and as ones perceived by observers as similar to themselves. This similarity may be significant in terms of race and gender. Basow & Howe, social learning researchers, have contended that "The social learning viewpoint states that children imitate same-sex models more than opposite-sex ones due to...perceived similarity to the model." (Basow & Howe 1980:559) Researchers have defined role models in terms of human examples whom observers can imitate and from whom observers can receive reinforcement. They have contended that role models go beyond providing simple technical "how-to" information, by setting norms and values, providing recognition and reward for achievements, and orienting behaviors on a certain course. (Almquist & Angrist, 1971)

Bell's investigations have led him to define role modeling in terms of two processes: identification and interaction. Identification with the role model by the individual involved any or all of the following: perceived similarity between the individual and role model, imitation by the individual of the role model, and assimilation by the individual of the role model's attitudes and values. Bell has contended that interaction occurred in different spheres of life. (Bell, 1970)

Social Learning Theory and Locus of Control

Social learning theory involves individuals' goals, expectancies, and social reinforcements. "According to social learning theory, man's behavior is determined by his goals. Behavior is always directional. An individual responds with those behaviors that he has learned will lead to the greatest satisfaction in a given situation." (Rotter 1971:58) Social learning theory has proposed that the probability of a behavior occurring is related to an individual's expectancy that the behavior will gain reinforcement and that the reinforcement has value to the individual. (Strain, 1993)

Bandura has defined social learning theory in terms of personal and environmental interactions. "In the social learning view, people are neither driven by inner forces nor buffeted by environmental stimuli. Rather, psychological functioning is explained in terms of a continuous reciprocal interaction of personal and environmental determinants." (Bandura 1977:11-12) Bandura has contended that the issue of locus of control as a behavioral determinant is related to reinforcement influences and to environmental stimuli. (Bandura, 1977)

Locus of control has been a valuable construct in studying many important attributes related to professional achievement. From the 1970's through the 1980's, researchers provided evidence of the following:

- Subjects with internal locus of control are more cognitively able.
- They are more mentally aware.
- Internal persons are better predisposed to learning.
- Persons with internal locus of control are more motivated than are persons with external locus of control.
- Internal persons possess more information regarding their status in certain institutions.
- They are more able to perceive relevant information.
- Persons with internal locus of control are more prepared to seek necessary information in experimental tasks than are external persons. (Erlund, 1984)

Rotter has asserted that persons with internal locus of control show more overt striving for achievement than do persons with external locus of control, who seem to feel that they have little control over their rewards and punishments. (Erlund, 1984) Deci, Weiner, and Parsons have seen internal locus of control as a facilitator of achievement in relation to attributions. (Deci, 1975; Weiner, 1972, 1978; Parsons, 1983) Researchers have contended that students who believe they could influence the outcome of their work are more likely to be motivated in academic studies. (Lefcourt 1981,1983; Strain, 1993)

An extensive body of literature supports the premise that students with internal locus of control show higher achievement motivation than students with external locus of control (Coleman, 1966; Weiner, 1978; Parsons, 1983). Research studies have supported the idea that individuals who score high on achievement motivation assume personal responsibility for their work and attribute success to something they personally do, rather than to luck or ease of task. (Crandall, Katkovsky, & Preston, 1962; Crandall, Katkovsky, & Crandall, 1965; Coleman, 1966; Weiner,1978; Parsons, 1983; Strain, 1993)

Locus of control research supports the hypothesis

"…that internals not only will show more initiative and effort in controlling their environments but also control their own impulses better than externals…it appears safe to conclude that internals, in contrast to externals, would show a greater tendency to seek information and adopt behavior patterns which facilitate personal control over their environments…"
(Joe 1971:627, in Erlund 1984:20)

Evidence suggests that those with internal locus of control

"…have a higher self-concept and are generally better adjusted, more independent, more achieving, more realistic in their aspirations, more open to new learning, more creative, more flexible, more self-reliant, show more initiative and effort in controlling the environment, are less anxious, have higher grades, show more interest in intellectual and achievement matters, etc.…It would seem reasonable then to try and aid people in changing to a more internal orientation, to help them realize the contingencies between their own behavior and relevant aspects of their environment…thus increasing the efficiency effectiveness of their behaviors." (Roueche & Mink, 1976, in Erlund 1984:19-20)

Evidence has suggested that persons with internal locus of control are more independent, cognitively able, mentally aware, predisposed to learning, and motivated than persons are with external locus of control. Therefore, it seems that the possibility of increasing persons' internal locus of control may be significant in improving their academic and professional performance. It appears that information concerning the relationship between internal locus in students and their observation of role models may be of further value. Evidence suggests that there is a relationship between locus of control in college students and their identification of role models. Evidence suggests that locus of control in college students tends to become increasingly more internal when the students have role models. (Howard: 1996:vii-156)

Further Review of Research Literature

The author, Dr. Lucinda Harman, and Dr. Stan Dyer of Central Texas College, and UMHB African American, performance studies students/alumni are conducting related research. Their investigations concern African American, college students at Central Texas College and their identification of role models. Measurement tools include a locus of control scale and the author's questionnaire related to the students' identification of role models. (See Appendices for tools to replicate this study.) The first purpose of this study is to investigate locus of control as a **changeable variable** in African American, college students. The second purpose of the study is to investigate the relationship of internal locus of control between African American, college students and the identification of role models. This study is built on a review of literature in the fields of education, psychology, industry, and labor.

In educational research literature, there have been two leading theories and many research projects directly pertinent to this study. Weiner has provided a theory of attribution, and Bandura has provided a theory of observational learning from models. Studies of many educational researchers support the ideas that having models can influence professional choices, academic and professional success, self-esteem, positive attitudes, and career salience in students and in professionals. Career Salience is (a) the degree to which a person is career motivated, (b) the degree to which an occupation is important as a source of satisfaction, and (c) the degree of priority ascribed to the occupation among other sources of satisfaction. (Lentz 1980:29, Masih, 1966) Career salience is a factor, which has been considered predictive of career orientation and probable career success. (Lentz, 1980) Finally, research has provided evidence of locus of control as a significant factor in achievement motivation and professional attainment.

In review, Weiner has asserted that people attribute their successes and failures to internal or external reinforcers. He has contended that internal persons attribute successes and failures to their ability or to their effort. Internal persons attribute their performance to causes for which they assume personal responsibility. External persons attribute their performance to factors for which they have no responsibility and for which they have no control. (Weiner, 1986)

Bandura's theory of observational learning has concerned learning from models. (Bandura, 1969) He has asserted that many behaviors are acquired through observing and imitating other people. He has contended that new patterns of behavior are learned through observing behavior without the observer overtly responding or receiving any reinforcements in the exposure setting. He wrote further, "Modeling influences…can create generative and innovative behavior." (Bandura 1977:40-41) He has argued that observers watch models performing responses, which embody a certain principle. Later the observers behave in a way stylistically similar to the model's behavior. Even though the observer is not mimicking the model's specific responses, the observer applies what he/she has learned from the model to a new, but related, situation. (Bandura, 1977)

Furthermore, Bandura and Walters have asserted that instructors as role models have three types of effects on students. The first is the "modeling effect," which involves the student's direct imitation of the model's behavior. The second is the "disinhibitory effect," which involves the student's observing the consequences of the model's actions and consequently choosing behavior in opposition, if the model's observed consequences are undesirable. (A current application of this concept might concern female or ethnic minority faculty members. If they are regarded with low esteem by school administrators and are not treated as equals, the effect may be to inhibit female and ethnic minority students' aspirations toward the teaching profession.) The third modeling effect is the "eliciting effect," which involves the increased susceptibility in a student to the influence of the role model. (For example, a minority teacher who holds high expectations for minority students' achievement may have an increased probability of influencing the students' performance through cues, which elicit a positive response in the students.) (Bandura and Walters, 1969)

Academic achievement has been related to the construct of locus of control in educational literature. Strain has studied locus of control as a predictor variable related to academic persistence and achievement motivation. She has asserted:

other educational researchers predict that...students with internal locus of control will persist longer in college...the findings of previous studies...warrant the conclusion that locus of control should be prominent in any current examination of motivation. Further, research findings accumulated over the last 20 years affirm the importance of locus of control as a factor in the motivation of students.(Strain 1993:6)

In discussing academic persistence and motivation, Strain has discussed internal locus of control as a valuable construct. She has stated, "...other than identifying locus of control as an important motivational factor, research has revealed little about the complex relationship between student motivational behavior and persistence in college." (Strain 1993:7) She has asserted that the process of motivation is complex but clearly related to locus of control. Strain has stressed that studying student motivation is important in that it is linked to student retention and achievement. She has contended that lack of motivation is associated with the withdrawal of students from college. She has argued, however, that although factors of intrinsic motivation are a basis for students' persistence behavior, only one, concrete, measurable, motivational factor, that of locus of control, has been identified in research. Strain has asserted that the construct of locus of control has been uniquely valuable in studying academic persistence:

...research conducted in the late 70s...conducted at multiple institutions with large numbers of students, reported findings that locus of control was related to persistence...All...studies found that students who were more internal persisted at higher rates.(Strain 1993:31)

The studies Strain has discussed have contributed major findings related to locus of control as a factor in persistence. These findings have defined an aspect of weak motivation and have identified "...a motivational factor which was amenable to intervention." (Strain 1993:31) Strain has contended that motivational theory is foundational to the study of persistence.

Strain has discussed motivational theory as that which aims to account for changes in activity. She has referred to the discussions of other researchers concerning motivation and persistence:

> "Intrinsic motivation relates to the character of the motivation that is described by goal commitment. Thus, an examination of the principles of motivational theory could assist in identifying factors of motivation that may be basic to student persistence." (Atkinson:1964, Atkinson & Feather:1966; in Strain 1993:30-31)

In summary, educational research has provided evidence of locus of control as a significant factor in achievement motivation. Evidence of this construct as predicting academic persistence and of role modeling as affecting academic success has also been found in educational literature. Further, educational research has provided evidence that role modeling by professionals affects self-esteem, professional choices, career salience, and professional success in students.

Studies in the field of psychology have also provided evidence of locus of control as a changeable variable, which is affected by modeling. Studies in this field have further addressed the relationship of modeling to change, the relationship of models to locus of control, and the relationship of investigation of knowledge (cognitive inquiry) to locus of control. Studies in counseling psychology have investigated the use of models to motivate change by observational learning. (Stebbins, 1975)

Dowling and Frantz have reported the results of a study designed to test the hypothesis that a facilitative model, one that communicates empathy, respect, and genuineness, enhanced imitative learning by an observer. The results provided evidence that "…if the counselor offers certain facilitative conditions …with a client, the client will be come more self-directing, more open, and flexible… " (Dowling & Frantz 1975:263) Numerous other studies in the field of psychology have also investigated internal locus as a changeable variable and as a variable which can be affected by modeling.

Stone & Jackson have explored the relationship between locus of control, modeling, and instructional effectiveness in a study using university students, divided into "internals" and "externals" according to scores on Mirel's factor of personality internality." (Mirels, 1970) Their studies have indicated that modeling is instructionally effective. (Stone & Jackson, 1975) Fry has also investigated subjects engaged in occupational information and vocational exploration. He has found that high cognitive inquiry, high "internal" subjects have made significant gains in all treatments but have learned most under a high degree of their own control of information studied. Fry has contended that the high internal, high inquiry subject types have had a better predisposition to learning; therefore, their gains have been superior in all treatment groups. (Fry, 1975)

In summary, literature in the field of psychology has provided evidence related to the following:

- Locus of control is a changeable variable.

- There is a positive relationship between role models and locus of control.

- A positive relationship between cognitive inquiry and locus of control exists.

- There is a positive relationship between role models change.

In 1994 in order to enhance understanding of the extent to which faculty's race, gender, and ethnicity affected student achievement outcomes, the ILR-Cornell Institute for Labor Market Policies sponsored a conference, "Role Models in Education." Six of the papers presented at the conference, entitled "Symposium: Role Models in Education," were published in the April 1995 issue of *The Industrial and Labor Relations Review.* In an introduction to the series, Ehrenberg presented an overview and review of the papers. He asserted that policies abound to increase the number of under-represented faculty in American schools and universities. These policies have been developed to provide employment for representatives of groups who have historically suffered discrimination. They have been designed, furthermore, to provide role models for minority students to enhance their educational performances. He stated that it is generally believed that increasing the proportion of minority teachers leads to improvements in minority academic performance and retention. He projected the hoped-for results of increasing minority faculty:

- Increasing the number of minority faculty at predominantly white institutions will improve the attractiveness of these schools to minority students.

- Increasing minority faculty will improve the possibility of minority students graduating.

- Increasing the minority faculty populations will stimulate the flow of minority students into higher education and into academic careers. (Ehrenberg, 1995)

In their conference paper on the effects of role modeling, "Do Teachers' Race, Gender, and Ethnicity Matter," Ehrenberg, Goldhaber & Brewer reported their findings concerning the influence of teachers' race, gender, and ethnicity on their subjective evaluations of their students. Ehrenberg presented the findings of Rothstein and himself that attendance at historically black colleges and universities (HBCUs) substantially increases the probability that African American, college students will graduate within seven years of starting college. This may be due to the greater likelihood of teachers and students being of the same race in HBCUs.

In the role modeling symposium paper, "The Effect of Attending Historically Black Colleges and Universities on Future Wages of Black Students," Constantine presented her findings that African American students who attend HBCUs receive higher earnings than they do if they attend non-HBCUs, in some cases approximately 35% more. Again this may be due to the greater availability of role models of the same race as the students.

Two papers from the role modeling conference, dealt with the importance of female faculty as role models in higher education: "Changes in Women's Majors from Entrance to Graduation at Women's and Coeducational Colleges" by Solnick, and "Do Female Faculty Influence Female Students' Educational and Labor Market Attainments?" by Rothstein. Solnick found evidence to support her theory that women who begin in traditionally female majors are more likely to shift to other majors, if they attend a women's college. She found that women at female colleges, where there were more female role models, were more likely to risk leaving female-dominated majors than women in coed colleges. She concluded that single-sex schools may benefit female students by providing them more flexibility to move into majors in traditionally male-dominated fields, that tend to be more rewarded in the labor market. In her study, the women's colleges yielded fewer graduates in female-dominated fields and more graduates in male-dominated fields than did the coed colleges. She stated, "Since wages…depend in part…on field of study…determinants of college major may further understanding of labor market discrimination." (Solnick 1995:513)

Rothstein addressed the low percentage of female university faculty in the United States and the possible long term effect on female students' advanced educational and market attainments:

> There is…concern that the percentage of female faculty at U.S. colleges…universities is too low…the New York Times (1993) emphasized this issue…that whereas about 20% of faculty…are women, the percentage of undergraduate women is more than double that figure. The question arises as to how female students might benefit from an increase in the percentage of female faculty. One view is that female faculty act as mentors and role models for female students, and thus promote their subsequent educational and labor market attainments. (Rothstein 1995:515)

Rothstein studied the question of the influence of female faculty on female, coeducational college students' post-graduate achievements using data from the National Longitudinal Study of the High School Class of 1972. The results of her study show a statistically positive relationship between the percentage of female faculty and the probability that female students will attain advanced degrees. She has stated

> The influence of the percentage of female faculty is especially interesting, because it may be that by acting as role models, or (indirectly) creating a favorable environment at the institution, female faculty may influence the career paths of female students. (Rothstein 1995:516)

In conclusion, literature in the fields of education, psychology, labor, and industry has provided evidence of a positive relationship between locus of control in college students and role modeling. Studies indicate that internal locus of control, self-esteem, career salience, and achievement in college students is positively related to the presence of role models.

Contemporary Research Design

Based on this evidence from previous studies, which are directly and indirectly related, the author and colleagues Dyer & Harman have designed a research study, which is an extension of the author's 1990's research (Howard, 1996), with college African American history students. (Tools for replication of this study are provided in the Appendices.) African American performers of African American autobiographies are performing for viewing audiences, which consist mostly of African American, college history students, via videoconference equipment. The sample population, which is the viewing audience, is reasonably homogeneous. The basic difference in the subjects of the sample is whether or not they identify role models. There is no controlled *treatment*. The comparison groups are those subjects who identify role models or not.

African American performers have been selected to perform historic role model characters from African American history. All performers have been identified as role models according to their demonstration of character qualities outlined on the role model questionnaire. (See Appendices) They are role models in themselves and perform, from African American history, role models displaying character qualities listed on the role model questionnaire (See Appendices). The historic characters being performed present an array of African Americans who overcame adversity throughout American history.

The presenters are performing and participating in discussions with the college student audiences following the performances. Discussion questions, asked by research facilitators from the delivery and receiving sites, are related to the characteristics identified on the role model questionnaire. (See Appendices) All subjects participating in this study are pre-tested and post-tested with a locus of control scale and with the researcher's questionnaire. (Howard, 1996) (Note that for purposes of validity it is critical that all participants complete the locus of control tool in its entirety.) In this research project, correlated t-tests, using ordinal statistics, are used to study the relationship of identification of role models to locus of control in African American, coeducational college students. (Howard, 1996) Preliminary results (with subjects who have ranged in age from 18 to 56, have been married and single, and have been freshmen-seniors) have supported the hypothesis that locus of control is a changeable variable. These initial results have also suggested a possible positive link, especially for sophomores through seniors, between internal locus of control and participation in the study.

Conclusion

Maya Angelou spoke of the importance of seeing role models:

"We need to see Frances Harper, Sojourner Truth, Frannie Lou Hammer, women of our heritage. We need to have these women preserved. We need them all:…Constance Motely, Etta Motten… all of these women are important as role models. Depending on our profession, some may be more important. Zora Neale Hurston means a great deal to me as a writer…If I were a black male writer, I would think of Frederick Douglas, who was not just a politician, but as a writer was stunning. In the nineteenth century I would think of William Wells Brown, Martin Delaney, and certainly David Walker…Richard Wright, Jean Toomer…Jack Johnson…Jesse Owens…Arthur Ashe…" (Angelou in Tate 1983:2)

In light of the evidence that role modeling can impact the achievement motivation in the observer who chooses to identify with the role model, writers/performers of autobiography (and writers and performers in general) should carefully consider the potential role modeling affect of their performances. Dan Sullivan of the *Los Angeles Times* wrote about solo performances:

"…it will be…about someone worth paying attention to, someone who made a difference…leave you feeling somewhat better about our chances for survival…We want to hear about people who thought they could do something about this world they never made. If Clarence Darrow could squeeze justice from the courts; if Will Rogers could blow the stage smoke away from the Government and expose the very ordinary people hiding there…maybe there's a chance for us…one leaves this type of evening feeling more nourished than is often the case of theatre of fiction…" (Sullivan 1975, in Young 1989:64)

Writers/performers of autobiography should make careful decisions about their presentations and choices of characters. They should consider the potential power and impact of the characters they present as role models. They should not underestimate the potential, redemptive, edifying power of their performances for social good.

Chapter Four

Researching for
Performance of Autobiography

Introduction

Elements, which have strengthened the endurance and potency of classic performances over time, have been noted from the histories of autobiography and of performance. Performances of classic, historic stories often present characters displaying the following characteristics:

- They exhibit fascinating, multi-faceted, paradoxical, or ironic characteristics.

- These characters frequently struggle with universal issues and significantly develop over time.

- Their stories reflect universal ideas and truths.

- They are commonly atypical characters from socially, culturally, or ethnically misrepresented or under-represented groups.

- These characters are typically pioneers who struggle with sociological and cultural barriers.

- They frequently effect the beginnings of the removal of these barriers.

- They commonly function as role models.

After the playwright/performer has identified a character with enduring and strong characteristics, he/she should look for a character with whom he/she, as playwright/performer, is able to bond. The performer should not just enact the character but should be able to empathetically become the character. Also, the performer's physical type should not usually be too far off from that of the character to be performed, as notable variance can be distracting. For example, Roy Dotrice was harshly criticized on Broadway for attempting to portray Abraham Lincoln because he was considered "too English and too short." (Young 1989:64)

Having found a fascinating, multi-dimensional character, the writer/performer should then study the historical setting of the character and his/her personal writing, such as autobiographies, diaries, journals, and other writings, which reflect the truth about the character's real nature and struggles.

Location and Setting

Visiting locations where the character to be performed experienced memorable events, which are related to the story to be told, may be very helpful to the development of the script and performance. Going to these areas to study them intellectually and to experience them subjectively may provide insight about the settings and about how the characters might have been affected by their surroundings. Writers/performers should go to relevant locations, if at all possible to study them and to intuitively and sensually experience the emotions, interrelationships, sights, smells, sounds, music, rhythms, and so forth in the atmosphere of the settings in which the characters lived.

When Hal Holbrook studied Mark Twain in order to perform him, Holbrook visited the places where Twain had lived to soak in the ambiance. As well as studying the details of photographs for Twain's gestures, mannerisms, attitudes, and emotions, he studied Twain's walk by shuffling up and down on the decks of ferryboats. He talked to people who knew or had observed Twain. He studied newspaper reviews of Twain's platform presentations. He reviewed accounts of Twain's appearance, delivery, and presentation techniques. He read reports of his casual style, which described him, as "puzzled, careworn…" and "[taking] in his audience…with a serious unconventionality." (Young 1989:73) After he read about Twain's smoking a cigar, although Twain never smoked on the platform stage, Holbrook decided to portray him with a cigar on the theater stage. The use of the cigar allowed Holbrook to *meander*. (Young 1989:73)

Primary Sources

Looking at the character as author, the writer/performer should look for original writings of the character, which are autobiographical in nature. Sometimes close, second-hand sources, such as interviews and biographies, by writers who knew the characters personally, provide interesting insights and lead writers/performers to first-hand sources. Primary sources enable the writer/performer to present real, human dimensions of the character. Only as the writer/performer develops an understanding of the character is he/she able to begin to develop a script.

Researching the original writings of the character to be performed can be an exciting adventure. Primary references, especially related to local histories, can be found in libraries museums, cultural centers, archives, or court records. Sometimes original sources can be obtained from living family members of the character to be performed or from the character himself or herself, who is still alive. In many cases, starting with library resources may be the best way to access first-hand material. Often libraries have special collections, which contain primary references. The research librarian can guide the researcher to reliable, authoritative sources in the library, in other libraries, and on the internet.

Internet Database Resources

The *internet* can sometimes provide valuable information from expert sources through accessing *electronic databases*. Researchers can go directly to relevant databases, which are organized, electronic collections of records, to access information *online*. Many periodical *indexes*, which are databases serving as guides to the location of periodicals, are available through electronic databases. *Abstracted indexes* include *citations*, *subject headings*, and *abstracts* (summaries) of articles or publications. Entire articles are not contained in indexes. However, *full-text databases*, which include complete texts of articles, essays, or books are becoming more available. There are databases within databases, which include *full-text articles*. There are systems of databases of academically reputable materials. These usually guide the researcher to *secondary sources*. However, in the bibliographies of secondary sources are commonly listings of *primary sources*. For example, researchers can find primary references listed in the bibliographies of biographies found through the biography databases.

In selecting a database or index the researcher should realize that some are *subject general* and some are *subject specific.* Databases and indexes can be geared toward different audiences. Some include only journal articles, while others also include books, government reports, and so forth. The range of dates covered and update frequency can differ. Some databases and indexes are published in English and some are multilingual. The introductions to these usually provide descriptive information about them. However, to use and *search* a database effectively, the following questions should be answered:

- Can a researcher search by *subject heading* (descriptor)?
- Can he/she search for keywords in *specific fields*, such as in the journal title or the author field?
- Can a researcher *limit* the search by language or by year?
- Can he/she find who holds the item? (Miller, 1999)

Once a database has been selected, the researcher can search the subject headings or *descriptor fields*, which have been assigned to the records in the database by professional indexers. These headings or fields are identified by d*escriptive terms.* These come from a list, *thesaurus,* of words used specifically for the database, in which all items on the same topic are described consistently. Researchers can retrieve all items on a topic using one term. (It should be noted that the same thesauruses or subject headings are not used in all databases, although there are some standard thesauruses. The Library of Congress Subject Headings is a standard thesaurus used in many of the databases.) Subject searching by subject heading can provide precision in accessing information.

After a subject-heading search, a researcher can search by *keywords.* Such a search looks for words or phrases in several fields, such as title, subject, abstract, and author. A keyword search usually retrieves more items than a subject search, but all the items may not be relevant. A number of irrelevant items may be retrieved because the computer looks for the exact word(s) typed, not for the meaning or context of the word. However, keyword searching is the best method in the following situations:

- Keyword searching may be used when there is no subject heading for the topic.
- It may be utilized when the subject heading is too general or specific.
- It may be useful when the subject is a new trend.
- It may be helpful when high recall and low relevancy is desired.

Keyword searching can be a starting place. It may enable the researcher to narrow the focus of research by retrieving a few articles that look promising. These articles could provide subject headings. (It should be noted that in many databases, a subject to be searched is referred to as subject heading or descriptor. A keyword in a search is commonly referred to as a *subject.*)

World-Wide Web Resources

To make the best use of one's time in using databases or search engines on the *World-Wide Web* over the internet, a researcher must define and limit his or her search. To begin a search the researcher must have a *research focus*, which is broken down into *search concepts*, described by a *research statement*. A research statement includes, therefore, basic ideas, concepts, and terms. In using the World-Wide Web, researchers may need to use various *search strategies* on different *search engines*. *Help* is usually provided for appropriate search strategies by the search engines. In general, a researcher can define, limit, or broaden his or her search, in using the internet, World-Wide Web, search engines.

A performer may want to study Martha Washington's personal conflict with the ownership of slaves for example. The basic research statement would be "Martha Washington's personal conflict with slavery." To effectively search for information related to this statement, the researcher should include the word AND or "+" between the concepts, which are expressed by keywords or phrases. Next the researcher should generate synonyms (BOOLEAN LOGIC) related to the concepts (keywords). A researcher could use a thesaurus to develop this list. Synonyms for *conflict* could possibly be the following:
problem, difficulty, dilemma, quandary, predicament, and perplexity. Next the researcher would type in the word OR between the synonyms. The keywords (synonyms) connected by OR would usually be enclosed by parentheses. Phrases may be enclosed by quotation marks. The example above might look like "Martha Washington AND (personal OR individual OR private) AND (difficulties OR problems OR dilemmas OR quandaries OR predicaments OR perplexities) AND (slaves or slavery)".

Most search engines allow *Boolean* searches, which involve the insertion of the words *or* and *and*. BOOLEAN searches can both broaden and limit the search for relevant information. Using phrases enclosed by quotation marks enables the search to connect the concepts (keywords). Some search engines recognize what is within quotation marks as a phrase rather than as separate keywords or concepts. Therefore, all the synonyms of a concept need to be connected together by "OR" inside parentheses. In some search engines the parentheses can further be connected by "AND" inside quotation marks. Where the parentheses are placed is critical, as most databases read the *OR* and *AND* in a particular order. (Usually *OR* is read first.)

Researchers should be aware that using general search engines on the World-Wide Web can have limitations. First, information is limited to that which has been published on the Web. There is also a lag between the time a site is published on the Web and the time that it is indexed. Thus, information could have been published on a website but possibly not yet indexed and not available to an internet search. Researchers should also be alert to the fact that some websites offer full-texts of canonical works in public domain.

Conclusion

Researching a character for performance is multi-faceted. It requires studying the historical, cultural, social, racial, and gender context. It involves visiting the physical setting in which the character lived, if possible. Most importantly, a good performance is not usually possible without a good script. A good script that gets into the subjective experience of the character is not possible without accessing the character's own words. Fortunately, today a writer/performer often has a proliferation of archival, museum, or library sources to access an historic character's own words. Even more fortunately today, most writers/performers have ready access to primary sources through electronic databases and the World-Wide Web. The best way for writers/performers to prepare to write or perform autobiographical scripts is to immerse themselves in the characters' own personal writings.

Chapter Five

Studying the Character

Introduction

In studying the original writings of the characters to be performed or sources close to them, writers/performers should look further for answers to the basic dramatistic questions of who, what, where, when, and how. Most importantly, the writer/performer should analyze the unique characteristics, which create the essence of the character. Contemporary writers/performers of autobiographies can be instructed by the techniques used by great solo performers in recent decades to reveal fundamental, unique, and/or essential qualities of the characters they presented.

Essence of the Character

James Whitmore said of his work in *Will Rogers' USA*, that his goal was not to photographically reproduce Rogers but to "capture the essence of the man." (Carroll 1977:1, in Gentile 1989:143) As Harry Truman in *Give Em' Hell, Harry!*, as Theodore Roosevelt in *Bully!*, and as Will Rogers in *Will Rogers' USA*, James Whitmore demonstrated in these three productions the power of suggestion to express the spirit of the character. Whitmore explained his approach:

"I have great trepidation trying to create what was so well known and so well liked…The main thing I strive for is to get the fundamental man, to recreate the rhythmic patterns. That's more important than doing an imitation…You just hope…to give a sense of the man…" (Whitmore in Young 1989:56)

Whitmore conveyed the impression of Truman with his characteristic grin, glasses, and quick speech. He presented the suggestion of Roosevelt with glasses, facial expressions, and a mustache. Again, his intent was not to photographically reproduce the character but to give a suggestion of him. Notable contemporary autobiographical performers have usually tried to present subjective, expressionistic portraits of the characters they are performing. (Young 1989:58)

Gentile stated "Just as the successful biographical one-person shows owe their acclaim to the characterization of the central figure, most of the shows that fail do so because of the weakness of the actor's impersonation or the inability of the script to capture the persona's elusive nature." (Gentile 1989:144) The script and the performance of contemporary writers/performers of autobiographies should reveal something of the subjective life of the character, not just the objective historical facts about the character.

Historical Accuracy

This is not to say that historic accuracy is unimportant in the script and performance. Virginia Woolf wrote about biography in her essay "The Art of Biography," that it

"…imposes conditions, and those conditions are that it must be based upon fact. And by fact in biography we mean facts that can be verified by other people besides the artist. If he invents facts as an artist invents them- facts that no one else can verify- and tries to combine them with facts of the other sort, they destroy each other." (Woolf 1967:225, in Gentile 1989:147)

Finding verifiable facts from first-hand sources may be a particular challenge with some characters, especially with marginalized people who present a somewhat fictionalized or elusive self in a public or social context. However, every possible effort should be made to glean information about the character from primary sources.

Juni Dahr of the National Theatre of Norway was concerned about historical accuracy in studying Joan of Arc for solo performance. To perform Joan even more complexly than Shaw's depiction of Joan allowed for her to do, Dahr studied original texts and actual transcripts from Joan's trials. In discussing her exploration of Joan's human side, Dahr stated

"She's not heroic. She was not a saint. She was not an angel. She had doubts. She's real." (Dahr in Young 1989:60)

Dramatistic Questions

Once the playwright has gathered such information, studying a character should begin with asking and answering basic dramatistic questions, such as the following:

- What motivates this character to speak and to act?
- What are the personal and cultural values of this character?
- What are the attitudes of the character? What are the demographic characteristics (nationality, race, sex, age, religion, social status, and so forth)?
- What are the psychological dimensions of this character (personality, mental health, morality, ethics etc.)?
- What does this person look like?
- What does the character do?
- How does the character move or act?
- What does the character say?
- To whom does the character speak?
- How does the character speak?
- Why does the character speak and act as he or she does?
- How does this character develop?
- What are the critical points in his or her life?
- How does the character respond in crisis?

Character as Specific and Universal

It should be noted that classic autobiographies usually have larger-than-life quality. The individual stories have cultural and universal relevance. The individual character remains identifiable, but universal meaning transcends the particular life. Often autobiographies present personae serving as role models. They frequently present characters providing advice and examples of both what to do and what not to do. This modeling is not only relevant to the particular age in which the character lived but also is commonly, universally instructive. Thus, the scriptwriter/performer might analyze what qualities about the character are both personally and universally significant.

Empathy

Performers/writers should seek not only to intellectually understand characters to be performed; they should also seek to empathize affectively or emotionally with the characters. Ronald Pelias defines empathy as "a qualitative process in which individuals understand and share the feelings of others." He describes the process of empathy as involving understanding the point of view of other, identifying with another, and adopting another's feelings. Empathy basically involves living in the world of another, moving from self-orientation to other-orientation and adoption. (Pelias 1992:87-88)

To become engaged in the process of empathy with a character, the writer/performer should understand the character's affective world. He/she should perceive the reasons for the character's feelings, attitudes, and values. The writer/performer should then attempt to connect with the character in terms of similar or shared feelings, attitudes, and values. Thus, empathy involves intellectual understanding and emotional communion. Further, it involves energetic commitment to the process. (Pelias 1992:94-95)

Following recognition and perception of the character's affective world, the writer/performer should seek to bond with the character in such a way that he/she becomes a part of the character's world. In immersing himself/herself in the character's own words and cultural, social, literary, and historic worlds, convergence into the character's affective world is facilitated. Writers/performers can involve themselves in projective identification by asking themselves how they would react *if* they encountered what the character encountered. They can ask how he/she would feel if he/she was in the situation of the character and so forth. The writer/performer can then adjust himself/herself to try to see the character's circumstances and relationships through the character's eyes.

Finally, the performer/writer must adopt the affective world of the character. Convergence is more involved with the emotions and adoption is more involved with the will of the writer/performer. Thus, empathy is a process of imagination and insight that happens over time, as the writer/performer immerses himself/herself in the words and life of the character and actively seeks to understand, converge, and adopt the affective world of the character.

In preparing to perform Mark Twain, Hal Holbrook used his memories of his own youth on his uncle's farm, when he described Twain's boyhood on a farm. (Young 1989:76) Alec McCown worked for sixteen months to learn his lines for *St. Mark's Gospel.* He developed his performance by tape-recording his recitation of the entire Gospel of Mark. He stated, "I found it impossible to listen to myself…It was formal, boring, lifeless, monotonous…" (Young 1989:35) Finally, McCown realized that, as he performed the words of a man of faith, he must exercise faith in order to perform the Gospel effectively. His recital of the book of Mark became one of the most successful one-person performances in the recent decades. (Young 1989:35)

Conclusion

Producer George Spota, a long-time advocate of biographical drama, gave good advice for autobiographical performers who study their characters. He stated

> "...four basic qualities are needed...consummate artistry,
> intellectual clarity, a sense of social ramifications
> of their character, and an ego flexible enough to let them
> get under their character's skin." (Spota, in Young 1989:67)

In summary, a writer/performer of autobiography should study his/her character by asking basic dramatistic questions. He/she should analyze and prioritize fascinating, significant, universal qualities about his/her character. He/she should pay particular attention to the character's specific, unique responses to critical life events. A writer/performer should seek to understand his/her character intellectually and to bond with the character emotionally.

Part III

Developing the Script

Chapter Six
Writing the Script

Introduction

The script should be driven, created, and built out of empathy with the character. The playwright can write scenes with emotional impact after he or she has listened to and understood the character in his/her historical, cultural, and social context. The writer of performance of autobiography should incorporate words and communication style of the historic character, which gives the language of the script uniqueness, color, authenticity, and intensity. Further, since "character is action," as stated by Eugene O'Neill, dramatic action comes through conflict and desire in characters.

Incorporating Action, Conflict, and Desire

The writing of the script usually begins with a critical experience or turning point for the main character. This crisis commonly involves counteraction of the character's desires. Conflicts with the desires, intentions, or motivations of the character can come from within himself/herself, from others, or from the character's environment. The opening, critical scene usually prepares the audience for what is to come. What is to come is typically foreshadowed. The focus is always on the character. The playwright develops a script, which enables the character to show his or her struggles. The script is written for action. In his guide to playwriting, Cassady wrote

> …characterization and action are the most important elements of
> of most plays. Once you know your central character, you know
> how the person is likely to react. Then you can place him or
> her in various situations and with various other characters
> to show these reactions. (Cassady 1984:ix)

The playwright should be careful with dialogue. He or she must know where the problem or tension is for the character. The playwright may write brief narrations, which can inform the audience; but primarily the playwright develops scenes, which visually show the struggles of the character. These scenes are ones of crisis and of significant action.

Developing Structure

Some scripts for autobiographical performances are like plays with plot, character development, and continuity. Some are more fragmented like montages or collages. Some integrate multi-media images, sounds, and images. Hal Holbrook explained his approach to his portrayal of Mark Twain as a platform presenter:

> "I have dearly wanted to get as much of Mark Twain on the
> stage as I can. But I cannot turn him completely inside
> out, as a playwright could be able to do, because I am

portraying Twain as a lecturer and he did not cry in public." (Holbrook in Young:61)

Autobiographical scripts, nonetheless, are usually structured works of art, which include a beginning, foreshadowing, discovery, incidents, crisis, and denouement. Scenes have rising action, climax, and falling action. The entire performance also has rising action, climax, and falling action.

The beginning of the script and performance is particularly important because the attention of the audience must be captivated and then sustained. Henry Fonda began his performance of David Rintel's *Clarence Darrow* with childhood reminiscences, which included hoeing potatoes on the hottest day of a summer. He said, "…and after I had worked hard for a few hours, I ran away from that hard work, and went into the practice of law, and have not done any work since." (Fonda in Young 1989:61)

Hal Holbrook designed his performance to capture and to sustain the audience's attention with humor in the first act. He said

> "My biggest desire was to make them laugh…at the start, so they'd go out at intermission and say, 'This guy's funny.' The second act became the social-comment section. In the last act, I gave them the Twain they'd been expecting all along; warm, whimsical memories of childhood. I think if I'd done the acts the other way around, the third act first, it would have killed it…surprise is the one thing you have going for you…"
> (Holbrook in Young 1989:77)

Pat Carroll described her concern for rising action and conflict in her performance of Gertrude Stein:

"...the first act...was absolutely on the button...The second act had to be re-written twice...If the first act didn't hook me and the second act didn't get me further along, I'd get up and leave...it has to have conflict, and it has to resolve like a regular play does...I don't want to play an entire two hours of anecdotes. There's no emotional involvement...If we believe in that marvelous thing that happens between live human beings... something electric happens...there's something that happens in the middle and it is electrical..." (Carroll in Young 1989:105)

Engaging autobiographical performances usually include incidents, epiphanies, and or experiences in relationships that promote self-discovery and understanding of self-identity. For example, even though some of John Leguizamo's characterizations seemed closer to caricatures in his 1999, one-man, Broadway show, *Freak*, his production seemed to primarily concern discovery of self-identity.

Being character-driven, the script enables the character to speak and to reveal his or her subtext through action. The motives, objectives, desires, or wants of the character are at the center of the performance. The playwright knows what is at stake for the character. And the stakes must be high. The audience is more likely to be engaged when the stakes are high.

Considering Point of View and Motivation

The playwright must determine the point of view of the character. The perspective of the character affects the selection and shaping of the character's speech and action. The speaker's point of view may be first, second, or third person. *I* or *we* characterize the first-person viewpoint. Implications of the first-person point of view include the personalization and presence of the speaker. This point of view focuses the listeners' attention on the speaker. The second-person point of view, often with its use of *you*, invites listeners' participation. The third-person point of view often employs *he, she, or they.* It is a less subjective point of view. The *focus* of this viewpoint is on others. Often the speaker is less personal. Each viewpoint uniquely focuses the attention of listeners. Each point of view establishes unique parameters in the speaker's relationship with the audience.

Performers/writers should also consider the issue of *credibility* and *privilege* in the point of view of characters. Characters who are not credible speak and act in subjective, unbelievable, untrustworthy, biased, deluded, or evil ways. Characters who are *credible* speak and act in generally objective, believable, trustworthy, and unbiased ways. Privileged characters or narrators have the inside story or private information. (Pelias 1992: 91-92) Omniscient narrators, especially in voice-over narrations, can be employed to provide information about the character from outside of a scene. The point of view of a character is revealed by the way the character expresses his or her thoughts and by action. Clarifying point of view is integral to answering the dramatistic questions:

- Who am I?
- What do I want?
- Where am I?
- Why am I here?
- When is this taking place?
- What is my physical life?
- What are the stakes?

● How badly do I want this?

The playwright reveals the strivings of the character with nature, himself/herself, and with others. The point of view of the character involved in these conflicts is revealed through non-verbal and verbal communication. The writer/performer should consider the character's point of view in his or her internal dilemmas, desires, and motivations. The playwright/performer should consider the character's point of view in interpretations of the characters and narrators. Point of view is also relevant to external issues such as non-verbal communication, visualization of the personae, pantomimic dramatization, and interaction between personae and the audience.

Choosing Form

Autobiographical scripts and performances can take many forms. They need not be exclusively written as factual, historic, prose, non-fictional accounts of a character's life. They can include virtually any written or verbal form, non-fiction or fiction, prose or poetry. Self-biographies, self-definitions, self-representations, self-revelations and so forth can be produced in many forms. For example, T.S. Eliot's poetry or Tennessee Williams' plays are autobiographical in nature.

Given the multiplicity of possible forms for writing and performing autobiography, understanding performance frames and voices for the one-person performance of autobiography is especially helpful. The three basic performance frames of the lyric, dramatic, and epic modes provide clarity for a wide variety of dramatic forms. In general, the lyric frame and voice is the most subjective. Within this frame the character speaks and acts out of subjective reality, whether it is real or fantasy. Generally, the epic frame is the most objective and ostensibly factual frame. (See Chapter Seven) In the dramatic frame subjective and objective realities and or fiction and non-fiction can be dramatized. The three performance frames provide clarity, which facilitates the possibility of presentation of multiple realities. (This discussion is expanded in Chapter Seven.)

Choosing the Known over Speculative

The playwright can write the script forward, backward, or back and forth in time. The script can move from reality to fantasy or back and forth. It can move from subjective to objective realities. The script can juxtapose more than one story. It is important, however, that the playwright/performer favors the "known over the speculative, the indisputable over the possible." (Pelias 1992:62) If verifiable information about a character has been difficult to obtain or if the character is particularly elusive or complex, questions about the character can be written into the script. More than one person's questions or perspective of the character can be incorporated into a kind of collage script. The perspectives of these different voices can contain both information and questions. Each voice, however, should incorporate the original words of the speaker whenever possible. Pelias asserts that a script which incorporates the original words of speakers allows performers a depth of understanding, an understanding much richer than if they would have just paraphrased what the other had said. To paraphrase is to reduce others. Saying the exact words of others in their unique form, in their complexity, in their style, in their intensity, helps performers to live in others, to share and understand worlds that are not their own. (Pelias 1992:96)

Historical Elements of Structure, Form, and Style

The study of classic aesthetic elements of structure, form, and style in the history of autobiography is instructive in developing an autobiographical script. Many classic autobiographies include dramatic tensions between competing external factions or internal conflicts. They often begin with narratives about childhood or youth, which are interrupted with crises, conversions, or turning points in the personalities. These critical periods are frequently revisited in retrospective narration. Turning points can involve shifts and developments in self-understanding, personal identity, maturity, philosophy, and meaningful relationships.

Out of careful selection memorable incidents are presented as scenes. These memorable scenes often involve obstacles, pivotal episodes, or epiphanies. The *epiphany* or *spot of time* can be performed in slow motion to reinforce the significant insights being revealed. Memorable scenes or moments can be revealed and/or reinforced literally, metaphorically, or symbolically. Truth and sincerity, however, in scenes are important values in most enduring autobiographies.

In general, classic autobiographies have included more subjective history of the writer's soul and more psychological intensity with more emphasis and concentration on significant moments. In contemporary notable autobiographies, an impression of a continuous present has commonly been produced, although the self of the autobiography is often dynamic, experiential, and changing. Contemporary noted autobiographies have presented multiple selves by way of more unified montage or by way of more diverse collage. Some include distancing in various kinds of codes or through fictional autobiography, such as in autobiographical novels. Sometimes dreams, fantasies, or myths have been juxtaposed with reality in contemporary acclaimed autobiographies or there has been a movement in these works between past and present. (Nalbantian 1994:1-37)

Relevant to recent developments in autobiography is Olney's contemporary theory of autobiography as that which presents the self through metaphor in prose and poetry. Olney has theorized that the self expresses itself through figurative constructs that transform the historic self into a *second self*. Olney has cited T.S. Eliot, as an example of this phenomenon:

"And heard another's voice cry: What! are you here?"
Although were not. I was still the same,
  Knowing myself yet being someone other…
  And he a face still forming; yet the words sufficed
To compel the recognition they preceded…
In concord at this intersection of time
  Of meeting nowhere, no before and after,
  We trod the pavement in a dead patrol."
  (Eliot 1943; in Olney 1972:304)

Olney stated that, as Eliot spoke in these lines, he was the convergence of the Eliot of the present, the Eliot of the past, and the Eliot of the future speaking in "another's voice" and surprised by his own voice. (Olney 1972:304) Nalbantian has theorized that past events were reinterpreted in the autobiographer's present awareness. Past events were related to present consciousness by way of significance. Specific elements of a personal history became universal, timeless, and poetic. (Nalbantian 1994:37) Likewise, Paul John Eakin has argued that autobiography is a psychological activity, which involves self-creation and self-invention. He has viewed autobiography as a re-enactment of dramatic scenes involving identity formation or as a "drama of self-definition." Olney and Eakin have suggested that even though the second self is presented through analogy, metaphor, symbolism, or fiction, the depictions of the present consciousness of past memory can be regarded as sincere and as true. (Olney 1972:304, Eakin 1985:34, in Nalbantian 1994:37-38)

In recent years, distinguished autobiographies have included significant sociological interests. Individual identity has been particularly representative of collective gender or ethnic identities. In such autobiographies self as a cultural construct dominates over the individual self-identity. In discourse related to these phenomena terms such as *other* and *difference* are common. A contemporary phenomenon of transmutation has emerged in autobiographical writing. Elements of one's self-identity have been projected on to the *many*, with which others can identify. (Nalbantian 1994:40-43) A transfer has taken place from personal to universal.

Other contemporary concepts of memory in autobiography include *generic memory*, *flashbulb memory*, and *engram*. (Nalbantian 1994:50) Generic memory involves the blending of personal memories into a generic image of common experiences.

Flashbulb memory involves specific, intense, immediate memories of the circumstances in which one first encountered a consequential event. Epiphanies seem related to this kind of memory. An engram is an auditory memory.

In contemporary autobiographies, close relationships, especially with family members, are often objectified and magnified into archetypal or universal relationships. Mothers and fathers are commonly seen as national archetypes. Scenes are frequently laden with symbols to the point that a universal situation is created. Literal locales are often transposed to metaphoric places. Visual and auditory impressionism is often employed, rather than literal reproduction. Chronological time is often interjected with subjective time. The past can be brought immediately to the present by a narration. Tunnelling and telescoping breaks down time barriers. Although transmutations of time are employed, chronological time can serve as a reference to tie moments of subjective time together.

The Manuscript

Writing and formatting the physical manuscript are not difficult for a one-person performance. Basic playscript format is appropriate. Each act begins on a new page. Acts are typed in all capital letters, underlined (ACT I), and centered. Double-spaced below the acts are the scenes, which are underlined and centered (Scene 1). Double-spaced below the scenes, the setting is next designated at the left margin by capital letters followed by a colon. (SETTING:) The setting is described by single-spaced sentences. Double-spaced below the setting, the activity on stage as the lights come up is designated at the left margin by AT RISE: and described in single-spaced sentences. Double-spaced below the description at rise, the designation of the first speaker is typed in capital letters and centered (MARTHA). Single-spaced below the persona's name and starting at the left margin, the persona's lines are typed. Stage directions can interrupt the lines, but they are written beneath the lines in parentheses, which are centered. (See Appendix C)

Once the script is completed it can be registered and protected by a copyright. Scriptwriters can obtain, free of charge, a copyright Form PA from the United States Copyright Office, by writing to the Register of Copyrights, Library of Congress , Washington D. C. 20559, by calling (202) 707-9100, or by visiting the US Copyright website at www.loc.gov/copyright. To obtain a copyright, the scriptwriter must return the completed form and script with a small fee to the Register of Copyrights. Instructions accompany the Form PA and more details are available in a brochure entitled "Copyright Basics," which is free upon request of the Copyright Office.

Conclusion

Although autobiographical stories can be performed in a multiplicity of ways, it is important to remember that the script for an autobiographical performance is basically about a character revealed through carefully researched and selected action, dialogue, and narration. Scriptwriters/performers need to study, understand, and adopt their characters and their original words. The character should be allowed to speak his/her own words in authentic and appropriate settings. Words, which are authentic, sensual, descriptive, and which have auditory appeal should be carefully selected and employed in good scriptwriting. The script commonly incorporates the following scenic outline. (Scenic frames, modes, and voices are discussed in Chapters Seven and Nine.)

- An engaging opening scene usually involves a crisis, turning point, or critical moment.
- Subsequent scenes build in intensity while revealing the unique history and struggles of the character.
- A critical problem or conflict within the character, with others, or with his/her environment rises in increasing tense action to a climax.
- The climax in the conflict is followed by action, which resolves the major problem positively or negatively.
- A strong ending with definitive action leaves a lasting imprint on the audience.

Multiple drafts, revisions, and edits are part of the standard process. In summary, Maya Angelou's discussion of her autobiographical writing with Claudia Tate is instructive.

"I try to live a "poetic existence."…I try for concentrated consciousness…Writing is part of my life…all of these other activities. They all feed into writing. I think is dangerous to concern oneself too much…with being an "artist." It's more important to get the work done…I study my craft. I don't simply write what I feel, let it all hang out…That's no craft at all. Learning the craft, understanding what language can do, gaining control of the language, enables one to make people weep, to make them laugh…studying my craft is one of my responsibilities. The other is to be a good human being as I possibly can be so that once I have achieved control of the language, I don't force my weakness on a public who might then pick them up and abuse themselves...I am responsible...I'm always trying to be a better human being, and second, I continue to learn my craft. Then, when I have something positive to say, I can say it beautifully...(Maya Angelou in Tate 1984:4-5)

In writing an autobiographical script, there is great room for creativity. However, the writer/performer must not forget that the performance will include the audience. The moments of the performance should be clear enough for the audience to enable them to respond appropriately. Using framing techniques can facilitate an appropriate response from the audience. Lyric, dramatic, and epic frames, modes, and voices can be useful in clarifying for the audience issues of perspectives, contexts, and relationships in scenes.

Chapter Seven
Using Performance Frames

Introduction

Lyric, dramatic, and epic frames, modes, and voices provide clarification for audience responses. *Frames* serve to organize dramatic experience. (Goffman 1974, in Stern:1993,5) They serve to unify scenes by setting them apart in a scenic context, as complete communication events, which clarify the *role* of the performer and the *role* of the audience. *Modes* establish the *relationship* of the personae (characters and narrators) with the audience.(Stern 1993:266) *Voices* involve the *communication*, verbal and non-verbal, of the performer, personae, and audience, which interact in a performance. These voices are unique in each of the three frames and modes. Thus, the form of the script depends on the frames, modes, and voices of the scenes. Playwrights can use three basic categories of scenic frames, modes, and voices: lyric, dramatic, and epic. (See samples in Appendix C.)

Language in Frames

The lyric scene is a private scene in which the character is alone revealing his or her thoughts aloud, as he or she thinks aloud, prays, speaks to himself or herself in a mirror, speaks aloud while writing in a journal or diary and so forth. The language in the lyric scene, frame, mode, or voice is commonly intimate or urgent. (Pelias 1992:57) The character in the lyric frame, mode, or voice uses *high context language*. That is, he or she frequently speaks in phrases or incomplete sentences, in a kind of shorthand or fragmented way. (These phrases or *beats* can be separated by three dots in the script to indicate where natural pausing would occur.) (Wolff:1988,103-104)

Dramatic scenes in which the character speaks to another very familiar person can also be in high context language. (Gray 1996:58) The character in a dramatic frame, mode, or voice can speak subtly through negotiation, manipulation, or implication with someone he or she imagines on the stage, speaks to offstage, or speaks to as a character in the audience. The performer as character can share a conversation with another imagined character. This can be done on a telephone or with an imagined character in an empty chair and so forth.

In the epic scene the performer, as himself or herself or as a character, speaks directly to the audience, as himself or herself or as a character. The language within an epic frame, mode, or voice is that of the storyteller or narrator. The script uses *low context language* with clear complete sentences in narration in the epic frame, mode, or voice. Further, the frames and modes of each scene establish the performer's relationship to the audience.

Relationships to Audience

One-person performance of autobiography can incorporate some interesting relationships and interactions with the audience. The reflective, lyric frame provides the most private, vulnerable *mode* for the performer as character; but it closes off the performer as character from a relationship with the audience. For example, Julie Harris as Emily Dickinson in

Belle of Amherst performed lyric scenes when she read or wrote letters or poetry aloud to herself. The audience viewed those lyric scenes through the imaginary fourth wall. However, the performers as lyric characters can move close to or through the audience without acknowledging them.

The dramatic frame or scene in dramatic mode, in which the performer as character interacts with a specific other, is closed in relationship to the audience as a whole. However, the specific other can be placed in the audience and the performer as character can move through the audience as he or she interacts with the specific other. The performer as dramatic character can speak to or with other imagined characters. In his performance of Harry Truman, James Whitmore shook hands with and chatted with imagined Herbert Hoover in the Oval Office. Later he conversed with the ghost of Franklin Roosevelt in an empty chair. (Young 1989:63) In *Belle of Amherst,* Julie Harris as Emily Dickinson spoke to her imagined sister and other characters. It should be noted that such techniques come across as contrivances in the work of performers whose imagination is not strong. Generally, if the performer as character intensely believes the imagined other character is there in the scene, the audience will also believe it. Julie Harris and James Whitmore are examples of performers who have been able to powerfully perform in the dramatic mode with imagined characters in solo performances.

Harris as Emily also spoke directly to the audience as rare guests in her home in epic frames in *Belle of Amherst*. The presentational epic frame and mode is most open in the relationship of the performers, as themselves or as characters, and the audience. A fascinating example of epic mode was

Alec McCowen's telling verbatim the story of the Gospel of Mark to the audience. McCowen did not portray Mark. Instead, he performed himself. In describing his epic storytelling approach, he stated, "I decided that I would simply enter with my copy of St. Mark, put it on the table, take off my jacket and tell the story-as if it had just been told me." (Young 1989:33) Even though McCowen performed St. Mark's text in the seventeenth-century, *St. James* version, he brought the story to life with present excitement by using the persona of a contemporary storyteller in epic mode. Gentile described McCowen's vital relationship with the audience as a storyteller:

> He wanted to give the Gospel an immediacy and vitality: his choice of persona…effectively cleared away the centuries separating the audience from St. Mark. The audience of the show did not move back in time…nor would it be quite accurate to say that St. Mark moved forward in the twentieth century. If McCowen wanted a fully contemporized Mark, he could have easily selected a more recent translation as his text. As it is, however, McCowen's *St. Mark* existed in a kind of time warp: first-century events, seventeenth-century language, and twentieth century persona and audience. Remarkable, the combination of time periods did not detract…the effect was the impression of universal timelessness. (Gentile 1989:164-165)

In the epic frame and mode, the performer can speak as himself or herself, can speak as a character directly to the audience (as characters do in soliloquies), or can speak as a narrator. The epic narrator can move close to the audience. The audience can become a group of characters. The audience can become people in a scene, in which the performer as character finds himself/herself in a social situation. In *Ian McKellen Acting Shakespeare,* McKellen performed Shakespeare in epic mode.

He said, "The atmosphere I'm trying to create is that of a party, in which I am the host and the audience arrives to meet the guest of honor, who is William Shakespeare." (Young 1989:83) In an "experiment- part autobiography…lecture…vaudeville…with Shakespearean poetry and drama…," McKellen began his performance by striding down an auditorium aisle and by springing onto the stage. (Farber 1984:17, in Gentile 1989:158) From there the "audience and actor were involved together in spontaneous dialogues and other kinds of stage business seldom tried on Broadway." (Robertson 1984:C11 in Gentile 1989:158-159)

In epic mode, Donald Freed, in *Villa,* portrayed a stone statue of the legendary Mexican general, Poncho Villa, which came alive and spoke directly to the audience in the imaginary context of the audience's dreams. Another interesting staging of the epic mode was *Einstein: The Man Behind the Genius* by Willard Simms. Larry Gelman began as the genius mathematician at a blackboard with his back to audience. He then greeted them saying, "My friends! I was so involved in my work I did not hear you come in." (Young 1998:62)

In the epic mode, the audience can be made characters, which enables interesting interactions for the audience with the performer. Making the audience characters in a social setting, with the performer as character, can serve to define the character in a social context. The epic frame or scene and epic mode commonly are the most engaging for an audience. In performing for audiences with limited attention spans and with limited commitment to the performance, the performer in epic frame and mode probably has the best potential for captivating them.

Frames and modes, which unify scenes and establish relationships between performer as character and the audience, serve to keep the character and the audience in the same place and time, and thus facilitate the imagination and appropriate response of the audience. Unrealistic and unbelievable time and place contrivances of context are not effectual for the relationship of the performer and audience. For example, a character speaking to a present audience from the after-life is not effective. Young recounts a *New York Times* review of *Mister Lincoln* performed by Herbert Mitgang, which described the one-man production as "'a banal fiction'- the president sitting in his box at Ford's theatre, describing his murder and telling the audience how 'my life passed before my dying brain.'" (Young 1989:62)

Conclusion

Given the multiplicity of forms, styles, and structures in which autobiographical stories can be told, the technique of scenic frames is especially helpful to audiences to enable them to follow, understand, and interact appropriately. Scenic frames provide contextual clarity. Modes also provide clarity, by providing parameters in the relationship of the performer with the audience in different scenes. The technique of scenic frames and modes enables the playwright/performer to present different facets of the character, which range across a subjective to objective continuum. Scenic frames and modes serve to keep the audience and performer together in the world of imagination and artistry.

Part IV

Performing

the

Script

Chapter Eight

Performing Subtext through the Body

Introduction

In writing and performing a script, a playwright/performer should consider non-verbal communication dimensions such as kinesics, proxemics, tactile communication, and object language, especially in the communication of the *subtext* (subjective reality) of personae (narrators and characters). How the personae would reveal themselves through gestures, movement, posture, facial expressions should be analyzed. Writers and performers should determine how the personae's use of relational and environmental space would reveal their conflicts, desires, and motivations. How characters would handle objects is a significant consideration. Further, how the personae would appear physically and how their appearance will reveal them is important.

Kinesics and Proxemics

Pelias defines kinesics as the study of gestures, movements, postures, and facial expressions. Kinesthetic communication reinforces or interprets speech. Kinesthetic behaviors communicate emotion. Pelias asserts, "Facial expressions are particularly powerful for communicating feelings. Research in this area has discovered twenty-three distinct eyebrow positions that indicate different meanings…" (Pelias 1992:74) Further, through kinesthetic behavior a character may attempt to control the speech or action of others. Finally, characters may use kinesthetic behaviors to care for themselves.

In seeking appropriate kinesthetic movement for the character, the performer/writer can observe and study people who are similar to the character. Performers/writers can also be guided by their own kinesthetic memories. Thus, empathy with the character and kinesthetic memory facilitates appropriate and authentic kinesthetic movement.

Kinesthetic movement and gestures must be carefully selected in autobiographical performances. Minimal character movement and gestures are usually better. Philip Baker performed Richard Nixon as a neurotic man who was coming apart. Of his performance of Nixon in *Secret Honor* Hall stated "I didn't want to do an imitation, I didn't want to do Nixon mannerisms." (Hall, in Young 1989:58) Julie Harris described Hall's work as a "masterful performance." (Harris in Young 1989:58)

Pelias defines proxemics as "the study of relational and environmental space." (Pelias 1992:75) It is affected by the degrees of familiarity, intimacy, commitment, comfort, station and so forth. Pelias describes proximity relationships in measured space:

> In intimate relationships, the distance between individuals when speaking varies from direct physical contact to about 18 inches…With friends…-a personal distance of about 1 ½-4 feet. With more formal relationships…a social relationship of about 4-12 feet. In public contexts…12 feet. (Pelias 1992:75)

Proxemics is a factor in people's relationship to their general environment, as well. Characters' spatial relationships to their environments may be affected by their status or physical, emotional, psychological, spiritual, or social well-being. These factors may also affect characters' spatial relationships with inanimate objects in their environments. Pelias presents insight about proxemics, status, environment, and objects. "In general, the more space they have under their command, the greater their status…Likewise, they may suggest their status by the quality and placement of their furniture." (Pelias 1992:75)

Object and Tactile Language

Characters can reveal themselves through object language. The way they groom, dress, and ornament themselves communicates their physical, emotional, psychological, spiritual, social, and cultural well-being; facets of self-identity, and dimensions of their relationships with others. These issues are, likewise, communicated in the way characters handle or relate to objects or props. The simple handling of a prop, such as a mirror or photograph, can reveal a great deal about the character.

The way personae touch objects, themselves, or others further reveals much about them. Pelias discusses the power of touch:

> Touching…is a powerful communicative act. The many common sayings in the English language associated with touch suggest just how powerful it is: we should be thick-skinned; we should handle people with care; we should avoid rubbing them the wrong way. Even a national telephone company urges us to "reach and out and touch someone." We see the power of touch most clearly by noting that infants who are not touched become ill and sometimes die. (Pelias 1992:76)

Body Positions and Movement

Basic principles of stage positions and movement are applicable in one-person performances. Body positions can be considered in terms of strength and use in frames. Full-front and full-back are very strong, although the later is used sparingly for obvious visibility and audibility reasons. Full-front is used most often in the epic frame. The one-quarter, angled, turned-out position is still strong, although less so than the full-front. It is usually used in dramatic and lyric frames. The profile and three-quarter turned-way positions are weak and seldom used effectively. (Dean 1989:61)

Stage movement can also be discussed in terms of strength. Strong movement includes straightening, sitting up, rising, putting weight on the forward foot, leaning forward, stepping forward, raising an arm and so forth. Conversely, weak movement includes lying down, sitting, slouching, stepping backward, placing weight on the back foot, stepping backward, turning around, walking away and so on. A moving figure is generally stronger than a stationary figure. Although the longer the distance covered by movement, the weaker it generally is. Movement needs to be intense and clearly motivated to be strong. Lines, subtext (subjective reality of the character), and mood can be strengthened or weakened by movement. Movement is executed on lines. An entering figure usually speaks immediately. Exits are usually on lines. Basic principles of acting and staging for plays are typically applicable in one-person performances of autobiography. (Dean 1989:146-182)

Conclusion

Characters react to their worlds according to their interpretation of events. The perceptions of the characters are revealed through their bodies, as well as through their voices. Performers of autobiography must consider how the personae would use physical business, activity, and movement to reveal their subtext and relationships with other personae. The writer/performer should move from empathetic perception and identification, concerning the internal and external elements of the character, to adoption and behavioral action. A writer/performer should translate empathetic knowledge of the character's attitudes, values, views, physical well being, and relationships with others into behavior or action that reveals and incarnates the character. This translation, representation, or incarnation is made easier by empathetic knowledge, identification, and adoption of the character and of the character's real, original, exact words.

Chapter Nine
Performing
the
Character's Voice

Introduction

The writing of the language of the script depends on the voice of the characters and narrators. Performers need to use effective narrative and character voices. Performers/writers should determine what vocal qualities are needed for appropriate voices and how these qualities can best be vocally delivered. The writer/performer must also consider in each scene the relationship of the voice with the audience, that is whether or not the voice in the scene is closed or open in nature to the audience.

Narrative Voice

If the script is to include a narrative voice, the scriptwriter may write a scene from the third person point of view. This narration would include language, which is written to tell or to describe rather than to show. The language of the narration would be written in complete sentences, which may be longer than high context, fragmentary phrases of lyric or dramatic scenes. The narrative scene could go backward in time, rather than forward or in the present. The chronology of the scene may affect the voices. The narrative voice is usually that of the storyteller.

Alec McCowen used a narrative, storyteller's voice in his production of *St. Mark's Gospel.* McCowen deliberately used the conversational voice of a persona who is a spontaneous, vital, excited, eyewitness storyteller.

"The operative word for McCowen is tell. He tells Mark's story, He does not intone it. He clears away the ponderous and Singsong preachiness of centuries of Bible reading to discover the urgent, living voice of a man who is recounting nearly contemporary events, many of them derived from eyewitness accounts." (Porterfield 1978:100, in Gentile 1989:164).

Character Voice

In order to determine appropriate voices for their characters, performers/writers should consider the point of view and credibility of the personae in their scripts. They should also consider the historic period, the culture, the status, the education, the dialects, the geography, the physical surroundings, and the health of their personae. To develop a character voice the performer should look for minimal characteristics of the voice, intelligible but suggestive of unique vocal characteristics. In performing Winston Churchill, Roy Dotrice used pliable pieces to round out his face and a dental appliance to push out his lower lip, which helped him produce unique characteristics of Churchill's voice and facial expressions. He explained his concern over not losing intelligibility, even though he went to such physical lengths to suggest Churchill's voice and face.

> "I think it would be terrible impertinence to imitate
> him literally- and it might not be good theatre, either,
> since he tended to drop his voice at the end of his
> sentences…which is just what you learn not to do as
> an actor." (Dotrice in Young 1989:58)

To determine voices for personae (characters and narrators), writers/performers should consider if the form of the voice should be literary, ceremonial, conversational and so forth. A performer, who uses an *elevated, standard, American dialect*, can produce a voice, which sounds formal, classical, educated, or trained. This dialect is between a standard American dialect and a British dialect. It has softer *r's*, more liquid *u's*, rounder *a's,* and is focused more toward the front of the face than standard American dialects. (Barton & Dal Vera 1995:184-193)

Dialects and Accents

A writer/performer should consider whether or not his/her personae would speak with a dialect or accent. Barton & Dal Vera define *dialect* as "speech specific to a certain native locale, class, educational, or social group within a native language." (Barton & Dal Vera 1995:134) They define accent as "pronunciation and style characteristic of a foreign language speaker." (Barton & Dal Vera 1995:134) In speaking with a dialect or accent, a performer should work toward giving an *impression* of the dialect or accent rather than a reproduction of it. Barton and Dal Vera state, "Many authentic dialects are incomprehensible…The actor's…responsibility is to be seen and heard." (Barton & Dal Vera 1995:253) The speech performer should study and practice dominant idiosyncrasies of the dialect or accent. As a speech performer incorporates these unique vocal qualities into his or her performance, he/she should strive to keep them consistent and therefore more believable. Dialects and accents can be studied by using dialect tapes or by listening to voices that present the dialects and/or accents on film, television, or in everyday life.

Vocal Clarity and Projection

Speech performers should also work at effective vocal delivery, which involves vocal clarity and good articulation. Vocal articulation is associated with diction, clarity, precision, intelligibility, and definition. (Barton & Dal Vera 1995:18) Articulation concerns the shaping of sound by moveable and immovable articulators. The moveable articulators are the lips, lower jaw, tongue, and soft palate. The immovable articulators are the teeth, gum ridge, hard palate, and throat. Effective articulation involves production of clear vowel and consonant sounds. Clear vowels are produced on open breath, which is unimpeded by articulators and shaped by the oral passage. Consonants are produced on breath and shaped by articulators. Properly produced vowels are open rich sounds. Properly spoken diphthongs and triphthongs, which are compound vowel sounds, are not overly elongated, as they often are in southern American or British cockney dialects. Properly produced consonants are not overstressed, as they often are in the American South. Good diction is facilitated when the voice is projected from the front of the face, not out of the throat, nor through the nasal passage.

Speech performers should work at effective vocal projection. Good projection of the voice depends on good breath support. The speech performer should fill his or her lungs and release breath as needed. Good breath support and utilization not only facilitates vocal projection but provides energy and eases tension. The speech performer should project his/her voice forward to enable even the audience in the last row to hear the voice without it sounding forced.

Vocal Variety and Resonance

Speech performers should work to develop vocal variety. As it is informed by the character and by the script, vocal variety can be produced with appropriate adjustments and variations of tempo, rhythm, pitch, volume, and quality. Vocal tempo is related to pace, rate, and speech. Vocal rhythm supersedes tempo. It involves tempo but also pace, pattern, pauses, accents, and stresses of syllables, sounds, and phrases. Vocal pitch is connected to inflection, range, intonation, intervals, median notes, keynotes, and range. Vocal volume is related to projection, size, power, intensity, dynamics, and audibility. Resonance, texture, tone, and placement creates vocal quality.(Barton & Dal Vera:16-22) Vocal elements are affected by the character's age, health, personality, status, culture, emotions, and relationships to others and his or her environment. Vocal patterns reveal insights about these factors. Vocal patterns can be symmetrical or asymmetrical to reveal the state of the characters. For example, they can be asymmetrical to convey anxiety, restlessness or fear. Or they can be symmetrical to convey regularity, formality, or confidence.

In order to engage the audience and to keep them captivated, the performer should establish justified vocal patterns that include vocal variations. A pleasing voice is usually flexible, relaxed, colorful, strong, liquid, expressive, and varied. Vocal patterns should not stay static but should build in intensity in the rising action of a scene. Vocal patterns establish setting, style, emotion, mood, and scenic development. Effective vocal delivery provides room for appropriate pauses, silences, or holds for laughs. Annette Bening asserts

> "One of the most useful effects I ever learned was holding
> spaces between words. When you…create…that…empty space…
> you create something…that needs to be filled. You have
> control. Everyone sits on the edge of their seats.
> It's dynamic." (Bening, in Barton & Dal Vera 1995:17)

There are three basic resonating cavities for the voice. One is in the front of the face but not focused through the nasal passage. One is in the back of the throat behind the uvula. The other is in the chest. A good speech performer allows his or her sound to resonate in all three cavities as the sound is moving and projecting forward. Vocal resonance gives rich, vibrant, and warm overtones to the voice.

Conclusion

Effective performance of the script depends on the vocal delivery of the performer. Noted Russian director Constantin Stanislavski spoke of some of the central elements of effective vocal delivery:

"After many years of acting and directing experience I arrived at the full realization…that every actor must be in possession of excellent diction and pronunciation, that he must feel not only the phrases and words but also each syllable and each letter. Our difficulty lies in the fact that many actors lack a well-rounded training in two important elements of speech; on the one side there is smoothness, resonance, fluency, and on the other, rapidity, lightness, clarity, crispness in the pronunciation of words. Words and the way they are spoken show up much more on the stage than in ordinary life…An actor should know his own tongue in every particular. Of what use will all the subtleties of emotion be if they are in expressed in poor speech?" (Stanislavsky, in Crawford 1995:41)

The writer/performer should determine how voice and vocal delivery will reveal the character. As well as carefully perceiving, identifying, selecting, and adopting elements of body and voice, the producer/performer of autobiography must carefully plan costumes, props, sets, and multi-media effects. He or she must consider how these will reveal personae.

Part V

Producing the Script

Chapter Ten
Production Elements

Introduction

I984 Barbara Rush began performing *A Woman of Independent Means.* This production, about a well-dressed Texas matron, ran for five months to sell-out crowds. The producers made what Rush called "a crucial mistake." Instead of keeping the production simple, they dressed up the stage with unnecessary backdrops and scenery. The stage manager of the production, Scott Alsop, contended

"The temptation with a one-person show is to load it up, make it look gorgeous. But the production can get too big- it makes the one person on stage look small, and takes the focus away from them…The simpler a solo show is, the better it is for touring. We have very intricate lighting, many changes of costume. The dresses are beautiful, but Barbara has to wear 75 pounds of layered costumes in the first act. Toward the end of the most recent tour, she began to wonder, 'Why can't we just put the lights on, do the show, and turn them off. Why can't I just do the whole thing in one dress?" (Alsop, in Young 1989:32)

Since the 1970's, especially with the application of electrical computer and theatrical technologies, support production elements have commonly outweighed and overpowered actors and their performances. One-person autobiographical performances with minimal costume changes, props, and sets have frequently been refreshing, effective productions of intriguing characters. Costumes, props, and sets which function as impression, suggestion, or metaphor can be powerful and impacting, even if they are minimal. In order for costumes, props, and sets to work effectively as impression or suggestion, they should have authenticity and truthfulness. (For example, in presenting Charles Dickens, Emlyn Williams went to great lengths to be as authentic as possible and had a lectern exactly replicated from the lectern that Dickens himself designed.) The changing and handling of costume pieces, props, and sets should also usually be simple and minimal so as not to disrupt the rhythm and flow of scenes in the production as a whole.

Costumes, Props, Sets

It is usually smoother and most effective for one-person performers to use simple, historically authentic props and costumes that can be changed with a simple piece like a shawl, jacket, hat, and so forth. James Whitmore developed three solo productions of famous Americans: Will Rogers, Teddy Roosevelt, and Harry Truman. In his performance of Rogers in 1970, he entered the stage as himself not as his character. He began his performance by speaking to the audience. He said, "If you look up Will Rogers in your encyclopedia…you'll find the following short note…" (Whitmore, in Young 1989:55-56) He continued discussing the entry as he took off his coat and tie, took up a rope, pushed a Western hat on his head, and began to chew gum. He spoke with a twang. While grinning like Will Rogers, he stood bowlegged. The audience loved it. The simple rope, hat, and gum along with the twang, grin, and stance provided enough of the unique characteristics of Rogers to create a suggestion of him.

Likewise, sets for one-person performances are usually easier to tour and most effective, if they are simple, historically authentic, and impressionistic. The approach to set design of acclaimed Broadway producer/director Hal Prince and of his great set designer Boris Aronson is instructive. Prince said

"Over the years Boris and I…moved further and further
from naturalism, from props and doors and tables…"
(Prince, in Ilsen 1989:101)

Aronson said

"I design from the inside of the people who inhabit the play,
not architecturally…Basically I am more concerned with the
nature of the script…the tendency is to do beautiful sets.
Some shows and their themes and characters don't call for
this." (Aronson, in Ilson 1989:143)

Prince was influenced by symbolism in Meyerhold set design. He has favored the use of impressionism and metaphors in his sets and staging. For *Cabaret* Prince split the stage into two areas. One represented the *real world* and one represented the *world of the mind.* Prince used a cold sterile set of metal and glass for *Company,* which served as a metaphor of marriage in Manhattan. In *Fiddler on the Roof,* the fiddler was perched on the roof as a metaphor of the Russian Jews trying to keep their balance in a precarious position. The impressionistic and symbolic set designs of Prince and Aronson have been good models for one-person sets, which need to be simple.

McCowen used multiple stage areas and the imagination of his audience to create the illusion of scenes in a variety of geographical locations. In *St. Mark's Gospel* McCowen's set and staging were simple but allowed considerable movement and use of the stage. His set was comprised of a table on which is placed a glass and water pitcher. At the table were three straight-backed chairs, which served at times as various objects, such as the seats of moneychangers in the temple, the stern of a boat, or a mountain peak. McGowen used different areas of the stage to depict various settings. He played the scenes in houses, in ships, and in the temple at the center of the stage, near where the table sits. He performed scenes in the street in front of the center area. The scenes by the sea were depicted even more down-center. The scenes by the mountains were rendered more upstage. The private or confidential scenes were played in a spot very far down front and so forth. (Gentile 1989:163)

Multi-Media Effects

Slides, video clips, projected images, sound effects, and music can all be easily used to enhance an autobiographical performance. If the multi-media projector is over the head of the performer, the performer can perform in front of images, which are projected from the front. Or the performer can perform in front of images projected from behind a scrim and so forth. There are many possibilities for performance with projected images. Special sound effects and music can also establish mood and believability in the audience. However, multi-media effects need to be carefully selected. There is a temptation with a one-person show to add too many multi-media effects or too much technical media spectacle. Sometimes overdoing technical or media effects detracts from the focus on the character and makes the piece difficult to tour. Usually the simpler a solo show is, given a good script and good performance, the better it is.

Young described an example of overdone visual effects:

Less well devised enterprises like Bill Studdiford's *Byron in Hell*- in which Ian Frost has been touring as the seventeenth century poet…-virtually reek with contrivances. The dramatist has set his subject in purgatory, flashing lights and all, and surrounded him with portraits… the stage is so cluttered with canvases Frost/Byron can scarcely move around, nor can he talk about anyone without displaying their picture…(Young 1989:63)

Models from Shakespeare

Effective staging techniques, which are especially applicable for simple one-person performances of autobiography, can be observed from Shakespearean stage productions. The greatness of Shakespearean stage productions in their time and today is dominantly in the script and in the characters. Stage realism is generally not desired nor attempted. The audience's attention is maintained in Shakespearean stage productions which move quickly, freely, and smoothly from scene to scene without disrupting changes of costumes, properties, and sets. Representational costume pieces, props, and sets engage the imagination of the audience. A doorway can lead in and out of one dwelling in one scene and in and out of another dwelling in is clear in lines from *Henry V*: another scene. The new abode can be indicated by a simple visual element or by an actor's line. A single branch in a performer's hand can represent an entire forest, again indicated by a line from the play. A few soldiers can represent a legion, a banner can indicate the arrival of someone prominent, or a few props can create the illusion of a lavishly decorated room. Shakespearean productions rely on the imagination and active participation of the audience. Shakespeare's philosophy in this regard

> Think, when we talk of horses, that you see them
> Printing their proud hoof i' the receiving earth;
> For 'tis your thoughts that now must deck our kings,
> Carry them here there, jumping o'er times,
> Turning the accomplishments of many years
> Into an hour glass (Shakespeare, in Carlson 1990:179-180)

Conclusion

By way of summary and conclusion, here are some tips for effective performance and staging of one-person performances of autobiography.

- Immerse yourself in the original words of the character.
- Remember that a good performance depends on a good script.
- Do your homework.
- Ask and answer dramatistic questions.
- Let the words of your character guide your emotion and movement.

- Use your emotional and kinesthetic memory.

- Be open and vulnerable.

- Use your intuition and imagination.

- Take risks.

- If you know it is not working, stop and begin again.

- Less is best.

- Keep it simple.

- Make it clear.

- Keep it truthful.

- Don't just try to be a better performer.

- Try also to be a better person.

Appendix A

Performing over Videoconference Equipment

To effectively perform over videoconferencing equipment, performers should do the following:

- They should adjust the speed of their voices and movement, as there is a bit of a time lag, when voice and visual images are digitalized over videoconference networks.

- Presenters should practice and rehearse their rate of speaking and moving with feedback from a viewer at the receiving site.

- Because the emphasis in any kind of camera work is on the visual elements, presenters should use interesting and varied visual aids without overkill.

- In order to engage long-distance audiences, presenters must be especially energetic.

- Communicators must be intensely involved in and committed to what they are presenting to captivate audiences at a distance.

Videoconference presentations can include the following:

- They can incorporate segues from performer to slides, photographs, or video clips.

- Long-distance performances, like those on-site, can incorporate audio-visual elements as visual metaphors.

- Videoconference performances, like those on-site, can include period music, sound effects, and voice-overs to engage audiences.

- As in on-site performances, long-distance performances can effectively included simple audio-visual effects.

Presenters of one-person autobiographical performances are able to communicate human interest and empathy over video-conferencing equipment. Technological equipment does not necessarily depersonalize performers, the characters performed, or the audience in the communication interaction, especially when the presenter is real and genuine and relates personally to audience members. Ironically, often the performers, characters, and audience interact more honestly and vulnerably over videoconference equipment than in on-site performances. Discussions between audience and facilitators at various sites and performers, which include questions on significant topics, typically follow the long-distance, educational, videoconference presentations. Often the audience members respond in a vulnerable transparent way, especially if the presenter relates to them as individuals. Many of the comments and questions from audience members are more personally significant than in on-site discussions. It is almost as if the videoconference configuration encourages an atmosphere of anonymity, which paradoxically encourages questions and discussions which are personal in nature, not unlike those among strangers on radio or television talk shows or those in internet chat rooms.

Performance and mass communication studies can be integrated. Corresponding to the revolution in computer technology, there has been an explosion in video technology, such as in the areas of videoconferences, long-distance learning via video equipment, educational videos and so forth. Presenters trained in skills of empathy and storytelling, as well as in camera presence techniques, are effective presenters and performers for video programming as well as for television and broadcast journalism. They are also able to effectively perform for multiple, long-distance audiences at once over videoconferencing.

In Texas, for example, BellNet, Bell County Network for Educational Technology, provides videoconferencing equipment for educational purposes. It connects community colleges, independent school districts, and other Bell County entities with each other and onto Texas' largest digital network, the Trans Texas Videoconference Network (TTVN) of the Texas A & M University System. TTVN connects over 90 sites. This videoconference hub connects with other hubs around the world. It facilitates long-distance learning and interactive communication. Performance studies students are effectively working and performing over BellNet, as well as in regional radio and television stations and video production studios. These students are becoming fine scholars and artists with skills that are practical and marketable. Programs, which encourage such training and opportunities, grow significantly in numbers of students and in artistic output, while gaining the respect and collaboration of regional communication and artistic institutions.

APPENDIX B

Guide for Introducing Speech Performance,
Through Writing and Performing Autobiography,
(On-Site and Long-Distance)

Goals-

1. Participants will demonstrate effective verbal and non-verbal communication skills for on-site and long-distance audiences.
2. Participants will examine autobiography broadly in terms of letters, journals, diaries, oral histories, and written autobiographies.
3. Participants will examine performances of autobiography.
4. Participants will use performance of autobiography as a method of inquiry.
5. Participants will use performance of autobiography to develop effective verbal and non-verbal communication skills for on-site and long-distance audiences.
6. Participants will demonstrate effective scriptwriting techniques.
7. Participants will become informed as critics of speech performance.
8. Participants will create a final performance of autobiography.

Group Requirements-

1. Participants are expected to attend each class session.
2. Participants will rehearse in small groups to prepare final performances.
3. Members of small groups are expected to coach and critique fellow group members in terms of the objectives of each session.
4. Participants will each give final solo performances, five to ten minutes in length.

Class Outline-

Week	Assignment (One week ahead)
Introduction to Course	Read Preface & Ch.1, Bring samples of autobiography for class discussion.
1. Learning from the History of Autobiography	Read Ch. 2. Bring scripts of performances of autobiography for class performance activities.
2. Learning from the History of Performance	Read Ch. 3. Bring list of historic characters to class to discuss in terms of potential role modeling effect.

3.	Choosing the Character in Light of the Role Modeling Effect of Performance of Autobiography	Read Ch. 4. Bring a list of historic characters to class to discuss in terms of research.
4.	Researching for Performance of Autobiography	Read Ch.5. Research a character original journals, diaries, autobiographies etc.
5.	Studying the Character	Read Ch. 6. Bring a rough draft for opening scene.
6.	Writing the Script	Read Ch. 7. Bring a rough draft for a 5-10 minute performance.
7.	Using Performance Frames	Read Ch. 8. Rehearse rough drafts.
8.	Performing Subtext through the Body	Read Ch. 9. Rehearse the character's voice.
9.	Performing the Character's Voice	Read Ch. 10. Turn in second draft for the 5-10 minute final performance. Rehearse second drafts.
10.	Designing Costumes, Props, and Set as Metaphors	Turn in costume, props, and set designs.

11. Designing Multi-Media Effects	Turn in a multi media design. Rehearse.
12. Performing over Video-conference Equipment	Rehearse.
13. Turn in final script.	Rehearse.
14. Run technical rehearsals.	Perform final scripts.

Appendix C

Script Format in
Sample Epic, Dramatic, Lyric Scenes

<u>Set Free!</u>

<u>Epic Scene</u>

SETTING: We are in a study at Mr. Vernon.
                                 The stage is set with a settee DC,
                                 a rocking chair UR, and a writing
                                 table and chair UL.

AT RISE: As the lights come up,
                                 the performer as a tour guide
                                 in a colonial gown
                                 approaches the audience from SR.

                          TOUR GUIDE
Welcome to Mt. Vernon. Today I will describe the life of the
lady of this house. In 1757, Martha Custis left the graveside of
her first husband, Daniel Custis. At twenty-six years of age she
inherited her husband's estate and became the wealthiest widow
in Virginia. Martha's life had always been marked by privilege,
but her adult life was also marked by pain.

                        <u>Dramatic Scene</u>

AT RISE: The performer as Martha is wearing a
                                 shawl over the colonial gown. She is
                                 standing by the rocking chair
                                 looking into it as if George is
                                 there.

                           MARTHA
George, I am worried. Why…riding on this damp, dreary day?
You're shivering…congested. I can hardly understand you. Yes, I
will see to the lame horse and the washout in the fields. (She
steps aside as if to speak to a doctor in the room.) Yes,
Dr. Craik, I understand that George has quinsy…his tonsils
inflamed. Our servant will go after your colleagues. (She steps
aside and calls a slave.) Billy Lee, ride to Alexandria to get
Dr. Craik's associates. Why are you hesitant? I need you to help
me. We may lose General Washington!

                         (BLACKOUT)

                        Lyric Scene

AT RISE: The performer as Martha Washington
                           is wearing a shawl over the
                           colonial gown. She is sitting at
                           the desk, finishing writing in
                           her journal with a feather pen.
                           She picks up the journal to read
                           her entry.

                           MARTHA
…Alone…outlived children…husbands. Servants…waiting for me to
die…to be set free. Slavery…repugnant to George. He did not
consult me…put his slaves' freedom after our deaths in his will.
So, here I am…in a frightening prison…afraid to be alone in any
room of this house…afraid to eat…could be poisoned…awoke this
morning with clear resolve…will go today to Fairfax County court
to sign papers to set free from servitude all of George's
slaves. Then I will be set free.

              (Martha rises from her desk and exits.)
                         (BLACKOUT)

Appendix D

Research Tools

Sample Participant Letter for Research Related to
The Relationship in College Students Between
Internal Locus of Control and Identifying Role Models

Dear Participant,

The purpose of this study is to identify a factor, which may empower college students academically and professionally. African American History classes at Central Texas College have been selected for this project. Your participation is voluntary and confidential. Your participation or non-participation in this project will not affect your present or future class standing, grades, or association with Central Texas College.

It should take you about fifteen minutes to answer the attached questionnaire and survey. At the end of the semester, you will be invited to fill out these same instruments again. Again, your participation is voluntary. The results of the pre-survey and the post-survey are to be compared. When this research project is completed, you are to be informed of the results of the project.

Thank you for your attention and participation, if you should choose to be involved in this project. If you would like to contact me in the future concerning this study, you may call…

Role Model Questionnaire

Definition of a role model-

In this study a role model is someone you admire. This person exhibits character qualities, which you would like in your life, such as in the areas of individual integrity, perseverance, personal success, communicational ability, organizational effectiveness, occupational satisfaction, and personal or professional achievement.

This person has positively influenced you in terms of your self-confidence, self-identity, determination, personal development, sense of professional direction, and/or achievement motivation.

Your name _____

Your address _____

_____ No, I do *not* feel I have identified at this time a
       role model as defined above.

_____ Yes, I have identified at this time a role model as
       defined above.

If you have answered "Yes," please check those of the following statements which apply to your role model. Please add any other statements that describe your role model or your relationship with him or her.

___ a. My role model displays individual integrity.

___ b. My role model exhibits personal success.

___ c. My role model has gained professional achievement.

___ d. My role model displays effective communicational ability.

___ e. My role model displays effective organizational ability.

___ f. My role model displays occupational satisfaction.

___ g. My role model displays determination.

___ h. My role model displays perseverance.

___ i. My role model displays personal achievement.

___ j. My role model displays professional skills.

___ k. My role model makes me feel good about myself.

___ l. My role model has encouraged my confidence in myself.

___ m. My role model has encouraged my personal dreams, ambitions, or goals.

___ n. My role model has influenced my personal development.

___ o. My role model has encouraged me to take my studies
more seriously.

___ p. My role model has encouraged me to be more serious
about my professional future.

___ q. My role model has influenced my professional or
career development.

___ r. My role model has encouraged my self-identity.

___ s. My role model has encouraged my achievement
motivation.

t. _____

_____

u. _____

References

Adelson, J. "The Teacher as Model." In N. Sanford (ed.)
    The American College. New York: Wiley, (1962): 396-417.

Anderson, R. & Ramsey, P. "Women in Higher Education: Development
    Through Administrative Mentoring." In L B. Welsh (ed.), *Women
    in Higher Education: Changes and Challenges*. New York:
    Praeger, (1990): 283-285.

Astin, A. W. *Preventing Students from Dropping Out*.
    San Francisco: Jossey-Bass, 1975.

Astin, A. W. "Student involvement: a developmental theory for
    higher education." *Journal of College Student Personnel*, 25,
    (1984): 297-308.

Baldwin, William. *A Myrrroure for Magistrates*. Lily B. Campbell
    (ed.). New York, Barnes and Noble, 1960.

Bandura, A. "Influence of models: Reinforcement contingencies on
    The acquisition of imitative responses." *Journal of
    Personality and Social Psychology*, 1, (1965): 598-595.

Bandura, A.. *Social Learning Theory*. Englewood Cliffs:
    Prentice-Hall, 1977.

Bandura, A. & Walters, R. *Social Learning and Personality
    Development*. New York: Holt, Rinehart, & Winston, 1963.

Barton, Robert & Dal Vera, Rocco. *Voice: Onstage and Off*.
    Fort Worth: Harcourt Brace, 1995.

Bean, J. P. "Student attrition, intention, and confidence:
    Interaction effects in a path model." *Research in Higher
    Education*, 17, (1982): 37-50.

Beadle, John. *The Journal or Diary of a Thankful Christian*.
    London: 1656.

Bell, A. P. "Role modelship and interaction in adolescence and
    young adulthood." *Developmental Psychology*, 2, (1970):
    123-128.

Berger, J. "Pessimism in air as schools try affirmative action." *New York Times*, 27, B1, 1990.

Bottrall, Margaret. *Every Man a Phoenix, Studies in Seventeenth Century Autobiography,* London: William Cloves and Sons Ltd., 1958.

Bretz, R. D. Jr., Milkovich, G, & Read, W. *Performance appraisal research and practice*. Working paper. Center for Advanced Human Resources, Cornell University (1992): 92-115.

Brockett, Oscar G. *The Essential Theatre.* Fort Worth: Harcourt Brace, 1996.

Carlson, Marvin. "Performing the Self." *Modern Drama*. 39 (1996): 599-607.

Carlson, Marvin & Shafer, Yvonne. *The Play's the Thing, An Introduction to Theatre.* New York: Longman, 1990.

Carroll, Margaret. "Stage Shows Can Be Singular Smashes." *Chicago Tribune*, 27 Jan. 1977, sec. 2:1.

Cassady, Marshall. *Characters in Action. A Guide to Playwriting.* Lantham: University Press of America, 1984.

Clemens, Samuel. *The Autobiography of Mark Twain.* Edited by Charles Neider. New York: Harper, 1959.

Colangelo, N., Dustin, D. & Foxley, C. *Multicultural Nonsexist Education*, Dubuque: Kendall/Hunt, 1979.

Commission on Human Resources of the National Research Council. *The doctorate records file.* Washington D. C.: National Academy of Sciences, 1980.

Constantine, J., "The effect of attending historically black colleges and universities on future wages of black students." *Industrial and Labor Relations Review*, 48, (1995): 484-485.

Crawford, Jerry, Hurst, Catherine & Lugering, Michael. *Acting in Person and in Style.* Madison: Brown & Benchmark, 1995.

Cushner, K., McClelland, A. & Safford, P. *Human Diversity in Education*, New York: McGraw-Hill, 1992.

Deci, E. L. *Intrinsic Motivation*. New York: Plenum Books, 1975.

Dean, Alexander & Cara, Lawrence. *Fundamentals of Play Directing*. New York: Holt, Rinehart & Winston, 1989.

Dickens, Mamie. *My Father as I Recall Him*. Westminister: Roxburghe, n.d.

Dowling, T.H. & Frantz, T. "The influence of facilitative relationship on imitative learning." *Journal of Counseling Psychology*, 22, (1975): 259-263.

Duke, M.& Frankel, A. *Inside Psychotherapy*. Chicago: Markham, 1971.

Delany, Paul. *British Autobiography in the Seventeenth Century*. London: Routledge & Kegan Paul, 1969.

Dweck, C. S. "Motivational processes affecting learning." *American Psychologist*, 41, (1986): 1040-1048.

Eakin, Paul John. *Fictions in Autobiography: Studies in the Art of Self-Invention*. Princeton: Princeton University Press, 1985.

Ehrenberg, R. "Role models in education, Symposium." *Industrial and Labor Relations Review*, 48, (1995): 482-485.

Ehrenberg, R., Goldhaber, D., & Brewer, D. 'Do teachers' race, gender, & ethnicity matter?" Evidence from NELS. *Industrial and Labor Relations Review*, 48,(1995): 547-561.

Eliot, T.S. *Four Quartets*. Harcourt, Brace, and Company, 1943.

Erlund, C. J. "Human Potential Seminar: It's Effects Upon Grade Point Average and Other Selected Characteristics of Community/Junior College Students," doctoral diss., East Texas University, Commerce (ERIC Document), 1984.

Farber, Stephen. "Enter McKellen, Bearing Shakespeare." *New York Times*. late ed. 15 Jan. 1984, sec. 2:17+.

Feedback Theatrebooks & Prospero Press. *Professional Playscript Format Guidelines and Sample.* New York, 1991.

Fitzsimmons, Raymond. *The Public Reading Tours of Charles Dickens.* Philadelphia: Lippincott, 1970.

Gerard, Father John. *The Autobiography of a Hunted Priest.* Translated by Philip Caraman. New York: 1952.

Gentile, John S. *Cast of One, One-Person Shows from the Chautauqua Platform to the Broadway Stage.* Urbana and Chicago: University of Illinois Press, 1989.

Goffman, Erving. *Frame Analysis.* 1974. Boston: Northeastern UP, 1986.

Gray, Paul & VanOosting, James. *Performance in Literature and Life.* Boston: Allyn & Bacon: 1996

Gray, Spalding. Letter to John Gentile. *Cast of One, One-Person Shows from the Chautauqua Platform to the Broadway Stage.* Urbana and Chicago: University of Illinois Press, 1989.

Gray, Spalding. "Preparing for Popularity: Origins of the Poet-Performer Movement." *Literature in Performance 6.* (Nov. 1985): 34-41.

Gusdorf, Georges. 'Conditions et limites de l'autobiographie'. *Formen der Selbstdarstellung.* Reichenkron and Haase, eds.: Berlin, 1956.

Howard, Diane "The Relationship of Internal Locus of Control and Role Models in Female College Students." Ph.D. diss., University of Texas at Austin (ERIC Document), 1996.

Ilsen, Carol. *Harold Prince from Pajama Game to Phantom of the Opera.* Ann Arbor: UMI Research Press, 1989.

Joe, V. C. "Review of the external-internal control construct as a personality variable. *Psychological Reports* 28. (1971): 619-640.

Katz, J. "Personality and Interpersonal Relationships in the College Classroom." In N. Sanford (ed.) *The American College*. New York: Wiley,(1962): 396-417.

Lefcourt, H. M. (ed.). "Research with Locus of Control." Vol. 1. *Assessment Methods*. New York: Academic Press, 1981.

Lefcourt, H. M. (ed.) "Research with Locus of Control." Vol. 2. *Development and Social Problems*. New York: Springer, 1983.

Lefcourt, H. M. "Internal versus external control of reinforcement: A review". *Psychological Bulletin*, 65 (4). (1966): 206-220.

Lefrancois, G. *Psychology for Teaching,* Belmont: Wadsworth, 1988.

Lind, L.R. (ed.) *Ten Greek Plays in Contemporary Translations*, Boston: Houghton Mifflin Company, 1957.

Lionnet, Francoise. *Autobiographical Voices, Race, Gender, Self-Portraiture*. Ithacca: Cornell University Press, 1989.

Maehr, M. L. & Archer, J. *Motivation and school achievement*. Washington D. C.: Office of Educational Research and Improvement. (ERIC Document Reproduction, Service No. ED 2659381985).

Mascuch, Michael. *Origins of the Individualist Self, Autobiography and Self-Identity in England, 1591-1791*. Stanford: 1996.

Miller, Jolee. *Databases: definitions and considerations*. Belton, TX: Reference and Public Service, Townsend Library. (unpublished document), 1999.

Miller, Lynn & Taylor, Jacqueline (eds.) "Performing Autobiography". *Text and Performance Quarterly*. 17 (4). (1995): v.

Misch, Georg. *A History of Autobiography in Antiquity.* trans. E.W. Dickes. Cambridge: Harvard University Press, 1951.

Mink, O. G. & Watts, G. E. "Reality therapy and personalized instruction: A success story." *Community/Junior College Research Quarterly*, 1,(1977): 389-396.

Montaigne, Michel De. *The Essays.* 3 Vols. Translated by John Florio. Everyman's Library, 1910.

Nalbantian, Suzanne. *Aesthetic Autobiography, From Life to Art in Marcel Proust, James Joyce, Virginia Woolf, and Anais Nin.* New York: St. Martin's Press, 1994.

Newcomb, T. M. *Personality and Social Change.* New York: Dryden, 1943.

Olney, James, ed. *Autobiography: Essays Theoretical and Critical.* Princeton: Princeton University Press, 1980.

Olney, James. " 'I Was Born': Slave Narratives, Their Status, As Autobiography and As Literature." *Callahoo,* 20 (1984): 46-73.

Olney, James. *Metaphors of Self.* Princeton: Princeton University Press, 1972.

Pantages, T. J. & Creedon, C. F. "Studies of college attrition: 1950-1975." *Review of Educational Research,* 48,(1978): 49-101.

Parsons, J. E. "Expectations, Values, and Academic Behaviors." In J. T. Spence, (ed.), *Achievement and Achievement Motives: Psychological and Sociological Approaches.* San Francisco: W. H. Freeman. (1983): 75-141.

Pascarella, E. T. & Chapman, D. W. "A multi-dimensional path analytical validation of Tinto's model of college withdrawal." *American Education Research Journal*, 20, (1983): 87-102.

Pascal, Roy. *Design and Truth in Autobiography.* Cambridge: Harvard University Press, 1960.

Pearson, Paul M. "Prominent Platform People, VI: Leland Powers." *Lyceumite and Talent.* (1980a) 13-15.

Porterfield, Christopher. "Telling Triumph." Review of
    St. Mark's Gospel, by Alec McCown. *Time,* 18 Sespt. 1978,
    100.

Pelias, Ronald. *Performance Studies, The Interpretation of
    Aesthetic Texts*. New York: St. Martin's Press, 1992.

Ramist, L. "College student attrition and retention." *College
    Board Report*, 81 (1). New York: College Entrance Examination
    Board, 1981.

Reinelt, Janelle. "Performing Race: Anna Deveare Smith's Fires in
    the Mirror." *Modern Drama*, 39,(1996): 609-617.

Robertson, Nan. "McKellen Turns Ritz into Globe: The Audience
    Participates." Review of *Ian McKellen Acting Shakespeare,*
    by Ian McKellen . *New York Times,* late ed. 24 Jan. 1984, C11.

Robinson, J. P. & Shaver, P. R. *Measures of Social Psychological
    Attitudes: Appendix B.* University of Michigan. Ann Arbor:
    Publications Division Institute for Social Research, 1969.

Rotter, J. B. "Generalized expectancies for internal versus
    external control of reinforcement." *Psychological Monographs,*
    80, (1 Whole No. 609), 1966.

Rotter, J. B. *Clinical Psychology*. Englewood Cliffs: Prentice-
    Hall, 1971.

Roueche, J. E., & Armes. "N.R. Basic skills education: Point
    Counterpoint." *Community and Junior College Journal*, 54 (1).
    (1983): 16-19.

Roueche, J. E. & Baker, G. A. III, & Roueche, S. D. *College
    Responses to Low-Achieving Students: A National Study.*
    Orlando: HNJ-Media Systems Corporation, 1984.

Roueche, J. E. & Baker, G. A. III, & Roueche, S. D. "Open door or
    revolving door." *Community, Technical & Junior College
    Journal*, 57 (5), (1987): 22-26.

154

Roueche, J. E. & Mink, O. G. "Helping the unmotivated student: Toward personhood development." *Community College Review*, 3,(1976a): 40-50.

Roueche, J. E., & Mink, O. G. "Impact of instruction and counseling on high risk youth." *Final Report* (Grant No. ROIMH22590, The National Institute of Mental Health). Department of Educational Administration. Austin: University of Texas, 1976b.

Roueche, J. E. & Mink, O. G. *Locus of Control and Success Expectancy (A Self Study Unit)*. Manchaca: Sterling Swift Publishing Company, 1976.

Roueche, J. E., Mink, O. G., Fisher, M., & Lindquist, A. "Impact of administrative climate, instruction and counseling on completion rate of postsecondary educationally disadvantaged vocational/technical students. *Journal of Vocational Education Research,* 4, (1978): 1-12.

Roueche, J. E. *Salvage, Redirection, or Custody*? Washington, D. C.: American Association of Junior Colleges, 1968.

Sanford, N. (ed.) *The American College*. New York: Wiley, 1962.

Satin, Leslie & Jerome, Judith (eds.) "Performing Autobiography." *Women & Performance, A Journal of Feminist Theory.* 10:1-2 (19-20), (1999): 9-13.

Schaeffer, Francis. *How Should We Then Live*. Westchester: Crossway Books, 1984.

Schlicke, Paul. *Dickens and Popular Entertainment*. London: Allen, 1985.

Shumaker, Wayne. *English Autobiography, Its Emergence, Materials, and Form*. Berkeley: University of California Press, 1954.

Shea, Daniel B. *Spiritual Autobiography in Early America.* Princeton: Princeton University Press, 1968.

Smith, Anna Deveare. *Fires in the Mirror: Crown Heights, Brooklyn, and Other Identities.* New York: Anchor Books, Doubleday, 1993.

Smith, Sidonie. *A Poetics of Women's Autobiography, Marginality and the Fictions of Self-Representation.* Bloomington & Indianapolis: Indiana University Press, 1987.

Spengeman, William. *The Forms of Autobiography.* New Haven: Yale, 1980.

Stage, F. K. "Motivation, academic and social integration, and the early drop-out. *American Educational Research Journal*, 26 (3), (1989): 385-402.

Stebbins, Emma (ed.) *Charlotte Cushman: Her Letters and Memories of Her Life.* Boston: Houghton, 1984.

Stern, Carol Simpson & Henderson, Bruce. *Performance Texts and Contexts.* New York and London: Longman, 1993.

Strain, B. "Locus of Control, Achievement Motivation and Selected Variables as Predictors of Persistence for Low-Achieving Students." Unpublished doctoral dissertation, University of Texas, Austin, 1993.

Sullivan, Dan. "One is Not the Loneliest Number," *The Los Angeles Times,* October 12, 1975.

Tate, Claudia (ed.) & Olsen, Tillie (preface). *Black Women Writers At Work.* New York: Continuum, 1983.

Tinto, V. "Dropping out and other forms of withdrawal from college. In Noel, L, & Levitz, R. (eds.) *Increasing Student Retention.* San Francisco: Jossey Bass, (1985): 120-140.

Tinto, V. *Leaving College: Rethinking the Causes and Cures of Student Attrition.* Chicago: The University of Chicago Press, 1987.

156

Wahls, Robert. "The Harris Mystique." Review of *The Belle of Amherst*, by William Luce. *New York Daily News,* 23, 4, May 1976.

Weiner, B. *An Attributional Theory of Motivation and Emotion,* New York: Springer-Verlag, 1986.

Weiner, B. *Cognitive Views of Human Motivation*, New York: Academic Press, 1974.

Weiner, B. *Human Motivation*, New York: Springer-Verlag, 1979.

Weiner, B. *Theories of Motivation: From Mechanism to Cognition.* Chicago: Rand McNally, 1972.

Weiner, B. *Achievement Motivation and Attribution Theory.* Morristown: General Learning Press, 1978.

Wolff, Jurgen & Cox, Kerry. *Successful Scriptwriting.* Cincinnati: 1988.

Woolf, Virgina. *Collected Essays.* 4 vols. New York: Harcourt, 1967.

Wright, Henry. *The first Part of Disquisition of Truth, Concerning Political Affaires.* London, (1616): 71-72.

Wright, Louis. *Middle-Class Culture in Elizabethan England.* Chapel Hill, University of North Carolina Press, 1935.

Young, Jordon. *Acting Solo, The Art of the One-Man Show.* Beverly Hills: Moonstone Press, 1989.

Diane Howard, Ph.D.

Dr. Howard, who lived her first years in Mainland China and Japan, has lived all over the world. She has performed, studied, and taught drama and music throughout the United States (including NYC) and in Europe. She graduated from a female college preparatory school, St. Andrew's Priory, in Hawaii. She earned her Bachelor of Arts degree in English and Music with secondary teaching credentials at the University of Oregon. She earned her Master of Education degree in Gifted Education and in the Performing Arts at the University of Washington. Finally, she earned her Ph.D. in Curriculum and Instruction and Communication (Performance Studies) at the University of Texas.

While teaching courses in personal poise and presence at Continental Career Schools as a college student, she was selected as Miss Eugene, Oregon and later as First Runner-up to Miss Oregon. In these capacities, she appeared in television commercials and special events. She has taught courses in Communication, English, and in the Performing Arts in public schools in three states. She produced a performing arts company,

Evergreen Performers in Tacoma, Washington. She was the artistic director for Arts in the Park in Manhattan, Kansas.

Dr. Howard is an associate professor of performance studies and communication at the University of Mary Hardin-Baylor, Belton, Texas. She has served as president of COMBRIDGE INC., a non-profit communication consultation corporation and is a presenter for BellNET. She has served on the board of directors for the Cultural Activities Center of Temple, Texas. She has performed at the Cultural Activities Center and at Temple Civic Theater, Texas. She has produced and directed touring productions staged at Temple Civic Theater, Temple College, and Central Texas College, Texas.

She is a published author. She has served as a reviewer of state grant applications for technology in education. She serves as a public speaker, performer, and presenter for civic and educational organizations throughout Central Texas. Her college competitive speaking and performance of literature teams have been state and national winners. She and her performance studies students perform one-person productions of autobiography in the Artists in the Schools program, which is sponsored by the Cultural Activities Center of Temple, Texas. She received the Sears Roebuck Award for Teaching Excellence and Campus Leadership for her work at the University of Mary Hardin-Baylor. Her peers nominated her as their university's nominee for the Piper Professor Award for teaching professionalism and excellence. The recipients of this award are to be announced in the spring of 2000. She serves on the steering committee for Performance Studies International.

Dr. Howard has presented her performance studies work at national and international conferences. In the Department of Communication and Dramatic Arts at the University of Mary Hardin-Baylor, where she has taught since 1988, she has developed a leading undergraduate communication, performance studies program. She designed a performance studies major, which provides training in performance techniques for theater, television, radio, and long-distance communication.

Dr. Howard's students/alumni are interns and employees in regional television and radio stations. They serve in cultural and performing arts facilities, videoconference sites, and video-production studios as interns and performers. Each performance studies student researches, writes, produces, and performs a one-person autobiographical production of a great historic or contemporary character that can be taken to theaters, schools, libraries, museums, and churches or can be performed for television, radio, film, or long-distance, live performance.

Having participated in educational research, curriculum development, and program delivery for BellNET, Dr. Howard has developed presentations and provided instruction on electronic research, computer presentation, public speaking, camera presence, and audience interaction over video-conferencing equipment. She has received administrative training in long-distance education from the Texas A & M Center for Distance Learning Research.

Dr. Howard's work is described on her web-site, http://www.dianehoward.com. The list (of approximately 100 pieces) of her performance studies students' autobiographical performances is linked to her vita and performance resume pages. Organizations with which Dr. Howard is involved as a scholar, researcher, performer, and presenter are also linked to her website.

Dr. Howard has three sons and two daughters-in-law and is grateful for their interest and support of her professional enterprises. Jon is a computer software consultant, designer, and programmer. Tiffany is the owner of a technical staffing firm. Matt is an entertainment, television, broadcast journalist and reporter. Jennifer is a history teacher. Mark, who has a website design business (Ocean Designs, which designed and maintains Dr. Howard's website), is completing college and preparing for missionary, aviation work. Dr. Howard's husband, David, is a marriage and family therapist. Dr. Howard expresses ultimate gratitude to her Lord Jesus Christ for His provisions, strength, and guidance of her work. She is grateful for the meaningful service into which her Lord has led her.